PORTRAITS OF
AMERICAN PRESIDENTS
VOLUME IX

THE
REAGAN
PRESIDENCY

TEN INTIMATE
PERSPECTIVES OF
RONALD REAGAN

Edited by

KENNETH W. THOMPSON

Miller Center of Public Affairs
University of Virginia

UNIVERSITY
PRESS OF
AMERICA

Lanham • New York • Oxford

The Miller Center

University of Virginia

Copyright © 1997 by
University Press of America,® Inc.
4720 Boston Way
Lanham, Maryland 20706

3 Henrietta Street
London WC2E 8LU England

Copublished by arrangement with
The Miller Center of Public Affairs,
University of Virginia

The views expressed by the author(s) of this publication do not necessarily represent the opinions of the Miller Center. We hold to Jefferson's dictum that: "Truth is the proper and sufficient antagonist to error, and has nothing to fear from the conflict, unless by human interposition, disarmed of her natural weapons, free argument and debate."

Library of Congress Cataloging-in-Publication Data

The Reagan presidency : ten intimate perspectives of Ronald Reagan ; edited by
Kenneth W. Thompson.
    p.   cm.-- (Portraits of American presidents ; vol. 9)
1. Reagan, Ronald. 2. Reagan, Ronald--Friends and associates. 3. United
States--Politics and government--1981-1989. I. Thompson, Kenneth W., 1921-.
    II. Series : Portraits of American presidents; v. 9.
E176.1.P83   1982 vol. 9
(E877)
973.927'092--dc21   97-1747 CIP

ISBN: 0-7618-0722-5 (cloth: alk. ppr.)
ISBN: 0-7618-0723-3 (pbk: alk. ppr.)

♾™ The paper used in this publication meets the minimum requirements of American National Standard for Information Sciences—Permanence of Paper for Printed Library Materials, ANSI Z39.48–1964.

To

those who search for a

deeper understanding

of the American presidency and presidents

CONTENTS

CONTENTS

PREFACE

One sign of the contemporaneity of the Reagan administration is the publication of five volumes on the Reagan presidency by the Miller Center. In approaching the Reagan oral history, we have reaped the benefits of participation by a larger number of witnesses and subjects than with any previous postwar presidency. With the Miller Center's Roosevelt oral history, no more than a half dozen high-ranking officials from that administration were available. With the greater availability of the Reagan official family, we have already exceeded 50 participants.

On the other side, we lack the authoritative historical sources, the monographs, and scholarly articles and the reconsiderations or revisions that enrich the study of earlier presidencies. No point is served in discounting the benefits of historical perspective. In the 1980s, this perspective is clearly lacking in the search for truth. With the Reagan presidency, if not all postwar presidencies, we approach a historical era the end of which is not yet in sight. We are dealing with a story viewed only from its beginning, its midpoint, and a few high points. At best we have only the most fragmentary knowledge of the consequences. Our task is the more complex because of the ideological divisions surrounding the Reagan presidency. Within and outside the administration, historians and scholars, as well as policymakers, cluster together around different value systems. Most important of all, a certain mystery surrounds the person of Ronald Reagan. Why was he effective? What were his unique strengths? What do his closest associates tell us about him? Did he understand certain problems such as the national debt?

The limitation of sources and possible observer bias are nothing new in the annals of political history. James Madison wrote of such limits, saying:

It has been a misfortune of history that a *personal knowledge* and an *impartial judgment* of things can *rarely meet* in the historian. The best history of our country therefore must be the fruit of contributions bequeathed by contemporary actors and witnesses, to successors who will make an unbiased use of them.

But Madison took heart from the fact that future historians and scholars might find in such early histories the sources on which more detached and objective studies could be written. His optimism about historical interpretation is one we at the Miller Center share. It lies at the center of our commitment to oral histories. We make bold to suggest that future historians of the Reagan administration will draw on these early findings. The participants in our inquiry have helped lay foundations for future research.

Madison concluded:

And if the abundance and authenticity of the materials . . . should descend to hands capable of doing justice to them, then American history can be expected to contain more truth, and *lessons . . . not less valuable*, than that of *any country or age* whatever [italics added].

INTRODUCTION

Fred Fielding was counsel to President Reagan from 1981 to 1986. Earlier he served as assistant and deputy counsel in the Nixon administration. He is a graduate of the University of Virginia Law School as a recipient of both the L.L.B. and J.D. degrees. He describes the effects on Reagan administration appointees of the Ethics in Government Act passed in 1978. It was the first administration required to conduct a transition under the Act. He was appointed counsel to the President despite not having planned to return to government. The legal responsibilities of his position as the President's lawyer included not only managing restrictions on what government employees could do on leaving government but also financial and personal interests on entering government. New public disclosure requirements were part of the Act not only for an incoming official but for a spouse as well. Fielding identifies what he calls the "criminalization of political debate," making recruitment for government service increasingly difficult. A highlight of Mr. Fielding's testimony, especially for the Miller Center, was his report on the status of the 25th Amendment at the time of President Reagan's assassination and of his cancer surgery. Counsel Fielding explains that no consideration was given to the invoking of the 25th Amendment at the time of the assassination, but when the President underwent surgery for cancer, action was taken to transfer power to the vice president temporarily but not through invoking the amendment and setting a precedent.

Kenneth M. Duberstein succeeded Howard Baker as chief of staff for President Reagan in 1987. He was earlier deputy chief of staff with a long history of working together with Senator Baker. Before that time he had been in the Nixon and Ford administrations. He entered the Reagan administration as the

President's chief lobbyist in the House of Representatives. Because the Republicans controlled only 191 seats in the House, Duberstein had to find support for Reagan policies from the boll weevil Democrats. He and his staff visited all 435 congressmen's offices to introduce themselves and lay the groundwork for cooperation on future legislation. They had a part in reducing the deficit and planning a budget. Reagan used the "bully pulpit" to reach the nation, especially through his Saturday morning five-minute radio talk. The President had only a few priority objectives: reducing taxes, spending, and regulation, and increasing national security. All of the major roles in the first year of the administration were focused on these objectives, with the exception of the Saudi Airborne Warning and Control System (AWACS). His overarching legislative goal was his economic package. He used the phone and met in half-hour sessions with members of Congress. He appealed to the grass-roots population of members districts when that was necessary to gain support for his Economic Recovery Program. Reagan was both a great communicator and a great lobbyist. Duberstein also cites the lessons he learned from Howard Baker when he returned as deputy chief of staff and ultimately chief of staff in the Reagan White House. He characterizes the work of the chief of staff as bringing all of the loose ends together. In one final observation, he recounts Nixon's advice to President Reagan on assistant George Bush's quest for the presidency, including a last-minute visit by Reagan to California.

For many years, Geoffrey Smith wrote columns on politics and world affairs for *The Times* of London. He contributes to the Reagan oral history by analyzing the relationship between Ronald Reagan and Margaret Thatcher. He finds it was the closest working relationship in history between an American president and a British prime minister. That relationship was vital to the decision by President Bush to act in the Gulf War. A habit of cooperation developed in the years when NATO was created, and the Reagan-Thatcher partnership renewed it following the postwar years when Britain appeared to have an inferiority complex. It had lost much of its prewar influence and power and with it the confidence that its views could gain a hearing in Washington. Mrs. Thatcher changed that in part because of the personal liking the two leaders had for one another and their ideological affinity. Smith views Thatcher as intellectually superior to Reagan. She allegedly commented to one of her advisers after an early postinauguration consultation with Reagan: "There's nothing there." The fact that Reagan was not consumed by vanity kept this difference between them from creating a problem. Also, Reagan supported her in the Falkland War despite U.S. interests in Latin America and the opposition of some of his advisers. Smith also traces what he considers Thatcher's role in persuading Reagan that they could deal with "the new man in the Soviet Union, Gorbachev." Without Thatcher, the deepening contacts between Reagan and Gorbachev would not have taken place, Smith concludes. He adds that she failed in two areas to have any influence on Reagan: on cutting the U.S. budget deficit and Reagan's idea or dream of a nuclear-free world. The British writer concedes that Reagan was unsurpassed in speaking without notes at an occasion such as the last meeting of NATO heads of state that he attended. On such occasions, he and not Thatcher was the dominant figure.

One of the liveliest and most spirited contribution in the Reagan oral history is that of the colorful Tom Griscom, assistant to President Reagan for communication. Griscom had been press secretary to Senator Howard Baker. He came into the White House when Baker became chief of staff. Griscom tells the story of Baker's selection of him as press secretary. He goes on to define the three critical elements of leadership: character, direction, and the ability to dominate an agenda. Reagan had all three. Communication was key to his projecting his views more widely than other politicians, David Broder once commented: He told the American people what he was going to do. He had a platform at the White House. He "walked into the TV era full bore." Often his visual image was stronger than his words. Griscom seeks to explain the sources of television's power. Reagan was able to craft a message that worked with television pictures. Sometimes the pictures tell the story, not the words. In part because of Iran-contra, he found communication outlets such as "photo-ops." It enabled him to control the message. The Oval Office speech provided another outlet that fit him like a glove. He used it and the weekly radio address as the principal means for communicating with the people. After Iran-contra when some were saying that his presidency might be over, Reagan was to get back out front through his skill as a communicator. Through communication, he lead the country. Finally, Griscom explains how communication advisers sought to help the President as in his dialogue at Moscow State University. Staff can assist the president in building on strengths.

Professor Shirley Warshaw is a leading authority on White House-Cabinet relations beginning with the Nixon administration. The focus of her study of the Reagan administration is on White House controls over policy-making, especially domestic policy. She points to a trend in every administration since Lyndon B. Johnson's presidency of exporting powers back to Cabinet officials. No White House staff existed before Franklin D. Roosevelt. As the scope of the activities of the federal government increased, the White House's role expanded. President Nixon campaigned on a promise to strengthen Cabinet government. He found that the various departments acted contrary to his wishes of reducing the federal budget. Cabinet officers were co-opted by their departments. In 1970, when Nixon created the Domestic Council by executive order, he set in motion a countertrend and revised the movement toward Cabinet government. Professor Warshaw concludes that President Reagan was most successful in forging relations between White House staff and the Cabinet. He sought to appoint people he knew and trusted. Pendleton James, who was a personal friend, did the recruiting with a group of Reagan's personal friends. Those selected for the Cabinet had interests in common with Reagan and were approximately his age. Three exceptions were persons whom Senators Paul Laxalt, Strom Thurmond, and Bob Dole urged on the President: James Watt, James Edwards, and John Block. Reagan sought to bind Cabinet members and White House staff more closely together through the Cabinet Council system and the Office of Policy Development. He appointed Dr. Martin Anderson to coordinate these efforts. He fostered loyalty through personal contacts. The basis of all of these initiatives was to control the policy process through the White House while maintaining cooperation and goodwill among Cabinet members.

After discussions of communications and White House control of domestic policy, the final chapter in Part II focuses on policy initiatives. Appropriately, the document on which the chapter focuses is a report dated 6 January 1989 from the secretary of commerce, C. William Verity, to Chief of Staff to the President Kenneth M. Duberstein. It summarizes some 25 separate initiatives by the Department of Commerce responding to Mr. Duberstein's challenge to make the last year of Ronald Reagan's presidency his proudest. The memorandum illustrates the ways in which a department can contribute to the success of an administration. Thus, item 1 is an initiative the effects of which are to cut the U.S. trade deficit while also promoting quality awareness on the part of American firms. Item 3 seeks to open Japanese markets to exports from the United States. Item 4 aims to prepare the United States for the new trade structure evolving in and through the European Common Market. Government 2000 recommends long-term goals and policy directives for the government in the year 2000. Item 16 involves the Census Bureau and preparations for the next census. Item 20 seeks to further a drug-free workplace based on cooperation between the public and private sectors. Telecom 2000 is a report by the National Telecommunication and Information Administration addressed to the requirements for taking full advantage of new telecommunications technology. With reference to policymakers, the challenge to the departments and presumably some outside groups originated in the chief of staff's office suggesting the monitoring of departmental activities from the center while preserving autonomy for the separate units in their choice of the next promising initiatives.

Dr. Otis Bowen had a distinguished career before entering the Reagan Cabinet. He was county coroner, a member of the Indiana House of Representatives, governor of Indiana, and professor of family medicine at the University of Indiana. He had been the first Speaker of the House, the first governor to serve two successive four-year terms, and the first physician to serve as governor. In the same manner, he became the first physician ever to serve as secretary of health and human resources. His tenure extended from 13 December 1985 to 19 January 1989. He had known President Reagan as a fellow governor. Dr. Bowen describes the program of HHS with a budget of $425 billion. The department's severest problems were AIDS, food-and-drug tampering, abortion, fetal tissue research, and animal rights. He writes about the reputation of the medical profession and maintains that the goals of government, the American people, and health care providers are approximately the same. Where they differ is in the realm of means. He discusses the health and welfare of the American people, and President Reagan and he were sympathetic to the need for affordable health insurance. Dr. Bowen was charged by the President to examine the whole area of private sector and governmental efforts to create and sustain health insurance. He recounts the way he organized the HHS study and how he made the case for the study before the Domestic Policy Council. The three areas the study explored were catastrophic health expenses of the general population, Medicare beneficiaries, and long-term care recipients. Dr. Bowen's rigorous approach to the problem and President Reagan's commendation of him for that approach illustrates the close working relationship of the two men.

Part III extends the discussion of governance to the international sphere, beginning with a discussion of international trade by Clayton Yeutter, secretary of agriculture in the Bush administration. Yeutter was responsible for trade, food, and agriculture policy issues while serving as U.S. trade representative in the Reagan administration. In 1991 he became chairman of the Republican National Committee. In his paper, he offers a comparative analysis of the two administrations in governance domestically and in world affairs. First, he praises the nation's ability to select the right president at the right time and applies the axiom to Reagan and Bush. Reagan was a leader with the ability to translate electoral success into policy. Yeutter uses his own case to illustrate Reagan's proclivity to be a delegator. He attributes the absence of much serious discussion with Reagan to the fact that Yeutter knew infinitely more about trade policy. Did it also reflect a lack of intellectual curiosity on Reagan's part? By comparison, the Bush presidency will go down as a less satisfactory one. Bush "was not in . . . Reagan's league as a communicator." He was not inspirational or convincing. He did not have a well-defined agenda. He lacked the personality characteristics to press his case, especially in domestic affairs and even in international affairs. Yet he had tremendous credibility internationally, based on experience. He was unable to translate his success in the Gulf War into legislative success. When asked what kind of president we need in the post-Cold War era, Yeutter answered, "a Nixon." By implication, Yeutter seems to be saying that President Bush with all his positive human qualities and wide international experience was not a president for the new era, a proposition that seems to contradict his earlier judgment that Bush was the right man for the times.

Sterling Kernek has twice been a visiting scholar at the Miller Center. He has written books and articles in foreign policy with special attention to the relevance of political realism for understanding hard choices in international politics. In a longer article, Professor Kernek applied concepts of realism to a series of post-World War II presidents. In the present essay, he concentrates attention on Presidents Reagan and Bush. While suggesting that Reagan embraced certain concepts that Morgenthau and others would have recognized, he points to contradictory elements such as a sense of limits versus ideological crusading and consigning Marxist-Leninism to the ash heap of history versus the idea of a nuclear free world. By comparison, President Bush's greatest virtue was restraint. He was somewhat skeptical of change in the Soviet Union, but he did not embarrass or threaten them, thereby encouraging them to give up their Eastern European empire. His decision not to oppose German reunification also suggested a realist perspective. At the same time, he succeeded in holding Germany within NATO, which both reinforced NATO and provided justification for the continued U.S. involvement in Europe. Certainly, one factor that influenced Bush's action in the Gulf War, and in particular the end of the Gulf War, was the need to maintain some kind of balance of power between Iraq and Iran. Although Bush spoke optimistically about a new world order, he also displayed a keen sense of limits, as in his policy in the breakup of Yugoslavia. He displayed balance and a blend of idealism and realism, combining Wilsonianism with realism in emphasizing that principle need not conflict with prudence. Bosnia proved the test case for his view of prudence, and even his critics agreed that the circumstances were not ripe for a decisive military intervention. Even though we hear mixed reviews of his policy on the ending of the Gulf War, President Bush's foreign policy was fundamentally a realist view. A discussion between Professor Kernek and four other scholars, including the French scholar Jean Marie Ruiz, followed the history.

I have included a brief commentary in the Appendix by John T. Connor, retiring CEO of Merck and Company and a member of Lyndon B. Johnson's Cabinet. In the Reagan administration, he served as a member of the Committee of Former Cabinet officials. His reflections are an appropriate, if somewhat critical, concluding statement for Volume V of the Reagan oral history.

I

PERSPECTIVES ON GOVERNANCE:
THE REAGAN PRESIDENCY

CHAPTER 1

THE REAGAN PRESIDENCY: A COUNSEL'S PERSPECTIVE*

FRED F. FIELDING

NARRATOR: Fred Fielding's association with the University of Virginia is longer than mine, and his involvement with the Miller Center is almost equally as long. He helped us when we undertook the subject of presidential disability and the Twenty-fifth Amendment and the selection of federal district judges.

Mr. Fielding is a graduate of the University of Virginia Law School, where he received both LL.B. and J.D. degrees. He received an A.B. degree from Gettysburg College. Mr. Fielding served from 1970 to 1972 as assistant counsel to the Office of the President in the White House and from 1972 to 1974 as deputy counsel. Currently he is a senior partner of Wiley, Rein and Fielding in Washington and has been a member of the Judicial Conference of the District of Columbia Circuit Court since 1976. Additionally, Mr. Fielding played an important role in terms of assisting younger scholars as a member of the Commission on White House Fellowships from 1981 to 1986. As counsel to the President between 1981 and 1986, he lived through and contributed to a historic period, so we are delighted that he is able to join us.

MR. FIELDING: Because I spent several years in the Nixon White House, I had a unique point of view or perspective going into the

---

Presented in a Forum at the Miller Center of Public Affairs on 28 February 1992.

Reagan White House. I served in the counsel's office in both administrations. Each experience was obviously different both in terms of organization and because the times were different. Furthermore, the politics in each era was different.

The perspective on the Reagan Presidency I bring is primarily that of a lawyer, although some people do introduce me by saying, "I remember when he was a lawyer." I did try during both administrations, however, to conduct my office and my operation primarily as a lawyer rather than as a purely political person. Because my observations will be primarily those of a lawyer, I may have to defer any questions on foreign policy unless they concern war powers. There are other areas as well in which I was not as involved as others were. One thing I should also mention is that I left the administration in early 1986, so while the seeds had been planted for what became known as "Iran-contra", it did not occur on my watch. Therefore I won't have much to offer on that issue, unless it concerns background on the individuals involved.

By way of introduction, I first became involved in the Reagan political campaign through a very informal group that Senator Paul Laxalt led called the "Thursday night group." Usually about 10 people—sometimes 20—met in Washington every Thursday night to discuss the campaign and make general observations about how the issues were being formulated. The group was very informal and included disparate sources within the Washington community from both Capitol Hill and the private sector, as well as people from the campaign.

My involvement in the administration began immediately prior to the transition period. By way of background, the Reagan administration was the first administration required to go through a transition under the Ethics in Government Act (1978), and many unanswered questions remained to be resolved. Many of its regulations did not deal specifically with the process of organizing a White House and an administration. The act had been passed during the Carter administration, and while the intentions behind it were good, the act was not well observed. The majority of people who left the Carter administration never filed the required exit filings, and no system had been established to enforce those procedures.

Before the election, a friend of mine from California, who had also been a colleague in the Nixon White House, called and said,

"Isn't there some new law, some ethics and government-type thing that we should be worried about when we win the election?" (I thought that was a pretty positive attitude.) I began preparing briefing books, not only for the incoming White House staff, but also for Cabinet candidates, so that everyone would understand what the act required.

I prepared the books prior to the election, but it was not until several weeks after the election that I received a call asking me to help. I went over the transition process, and we created an office called the Conflicts of Interest Council. It then became my task to screen for conflicts of interest and enforce the Ethics and Government Act, first at the Cabinet level, then at the levels of the sub-Cabinet, all presidential appointees, and commissioned White House staff people.

No one really knew how things should be working. No guidelines existed for what one should do in this kind of situation. I brought someone over from the Office of Government Ethics and had them detailed to my office so that I at least would have a liaison with the Office of Government Ethics. We worked out the problems and improvised as we went. It was easy for me to be relatively hard on people because I had announced that I was not going into government and could therefore act with total impunity: I could tell people that they had to do certain things and that they had to sell certain assets without worrying about whom I might or might not offend.

With the Cabinet, we went through a very intense period because the Senate wanted to confirm or pre-hear the entire Cabinet so that everyone could be sworn in the day after the inauguration. Confirmation hearings were held on people before the administration took office. An interesting sidelight to this was the Ray Donovan situation. We reached a stage when the entire Cabinet had been confirmed except for Labor Secretary-designee Donovan, who at the last minute had been the subject of several accusations about ties to organized crime. We had to go through a very intense procedure of updating FBI reports, and at one point we had a situation where the FBI was delivering reports upon which a judgment was supposed to be made by the President as to whether he wanted to go forward with the candidate. However, both the President and the Senate committee were receiving these reports simultaneously. It was an aberration that caused a great deal of confusion as to who knew what information and, later, hearings *ad nauseam* in the Senate. Very simply, the system wasn't prepared for the situation, and it went askew.

On Inauguration Day, we weren't even close to finished clearing the sub-Cabinet, and I was asked to stay temporarily until the new counsel to the President was appointed. I kept asking who the new counsel to the President was because I had to return to my law practice. A couple of days later, the President called and asked if I would take the job. I told him that I really had not planned on going into government and that others were ready to take the job. In addition to that reasoning, I certainly couldn't commit myself for four years, and I believed that anyone who did go into the White House should commit to the President for the full term, at his pleasure, of course. The President, however, said that we could worry about that "four-years thing" later; I accepted on that condition. Ironically, I was with the administration for almost six years and was the only original member of the White House senior staff who stayed that long.

In this discussion I would like to dwell primarily on the legal aspects of my position because that is basically the area where my responsibilities were involved . This discussion can also touch on the judicial selection process that evolved during that period of time. It is also important to recall that one of the most significant things a counsel to the President must remember—that is, you are counsel to the president *as president* and to the institution of the presidency. This distinction is vital.

QUESTION: I remember that in the Office of General Counsel in the Navy, a man wrote a memorandum for us on the ethics statutes as they were at that time. As I recall, they primarily involved things that one could not do after leaving the government, on account of having been in the government. I take it that the modern ethics and government acts have more to do with what a person can own when entering government. Could you provide a sketch of what the new acts involve?

MR. FIELDING: Restrictions on what one was not allowed to do upon leaving government have always existed. For instance, a person could never and still cannot work directly with the government on a matter in which that person had been directly involved with when in the government. That rule, of course, leads to definitional issues of what constitutes a particular matter.

While restrictions have always been in place for postgovernment employment, the new problems concerned people entering government. The new Ethics in Government Act placed restrictions on what one could own and what one's financial and personal interests could be. There has always been a certain amount of that type of restriction. Everyone remembers the David Packard situation, where Mr. Packard had to devise some very involved trust fund arrangements when he was nominated to be secretary of defense.

Under the new act, however, the rules were broadened and made more specific across the entire government. Additionally, many public disclosure requirements were imposed, and many people who were coming into the administration questioned why they should disclose that information when no one had ever been required to do so before. Some people entering the administration were also much more conservative in their outlook and felt that these requirements were intrusive.

I have heard many people say, "I don't mind telling you, but why should everyone in my neighborhood know?" Some of their reasoning was philosophical, and some of it was very practical. Some of these people had lived their lives modestly and had raised their children in their own way. They did not necessarily want their children to be known by others as rich kids, or they didn't want their kids to know they were rich kids.

For some people, the community thought were doing pretty well, but they were not doing that well. Some people were involved in partnerships in smaller communities with people, and that was their private business. In that era, however, people were concerned that they might be exposing their families to kidnapping threats and that sort of thing. So there were more than just philosophical or selfish reasons for why people didn't want to disclose their financial status. In addition, in many instances divestitures that were very expensive for people were required. They had to pay on capital gains, for instance, which they weren't anticipating, in addition to taking the huge salary cuts people often incur when entering government service.

Finally, the requirements involved not only the person going into government, but also his or her spouse. That situation caused a little friction. At times very qualified people were interested in government positions—at the Department of Housing and Urban Development (HUD), for instance—but could not take the job because they were not able to extricate themselves from real estate and limited partnerships, while others could not do so without causing their partners tremendous expense. So a number of problems arose that no one had ever confronted.

The financial disclosure issue caused a lot of people to say, "It's not worth it." My concern, especially on divestiture, was that there was no way to protect a person. Early on, we proposed an amendment to the Ethics in Government Act that would allow for the deferment of capital gains, as long as that money was put into a suitable investment. The theory was that a government officer would defer any capital gain, just as he or she would do with a home, until the next time that investment was sold. The amendment was not enacted until two years ago, but now that it has been, it is a good thing. I must say that the worst thing about the Ethics in Government Act is the title. Who is politically brave enough to say that it is time to amend the Ethics in Government Act?

No one had thought through these kinds of problems, and we had to deal with them as best we could. For example, there is a period of 30 days before financial information is subject to public disclosure. After that period, anyone who alleges to have an interest can apply for a copy of a financial statement. Our problem was that we were trying to pre-clear people, so they were filling out their forms and signing them before they even had a confirmation hearing. We dealt with this problem by having people submit their forms, but with "draft" written on them and leaving them unsigned.

The Ethics in Government Act has many good qualities, but one should not be afraid to change something just because of its title. One should not be afraid to look at the effectiveness of an act to see where any deficiencies might occur so that they can be corrected. If an act that is supposed to ensure quality in government becomes an instrument that denies the people who are most qualified to govern, then the purpose of the act is diminished. If I sound like a preacher, it is because I have been preaching on the act for some time.

I was very pleased that President Bush's first executive order created a bipartisan review commission of the Ethics in Government Act, on which I had the pleasure of serving. The commission came into being because of changes such as the deferment amendment that I mentioned. It also resulted from another problem: The legislative branch had imposed restrictions on the executive branch, but the legislative branch was under no similar restrictions. I can safely say that the American public has witnessed a breakdown in comity between the executive and legislative branches; in addition, it has witnessed what is in a certain respect the anarchy of the committees and a proliferation of committees, subcommittees, and sub-subcommittees on the Hill.

The early 1980s were also the beginning of what one could call the "criminalization of political debate," which again made it very difficult to recruit people for government. Some people entered government with the greatest of ideas but without good political sense, and they may have acted with bad judgment. Their actions, however, instead of being acknowledged as resulting from an error in judgment or maybe even stupidity, were somehow characterized as being venal, and these persons were subjected to bitter oversight committee hearings. When these persons return to the private sector and someone during a business meeting says, "The President wants me to do *XYZ*," the former government officials are going to advise them not to do it, saying that they will ruin their reputation by doing so. This situation creates a serious problem for people in government.

NARRATOR: Did you lose anyone because of this problem?

MR. FIELDING: We lost many people in the recruiting process, but it is difficult to quantify it in any particular way because one never knows at what level one loses them. Some may have turned down positions immediately because they were aware of the restrictions. Others may have done so after they got further into the process. Some people probably also used the restrictions as an excuse. In answer to your question, we lost many people, and the government is still losing people.

QUESTION: Recently, an informative seminar was held at the Miller Center on the disability of Woodrow Wilson in 1919 and 1920. At that time, there was apparently little statutory guidance on presidential disability, and what did exist compelled neither a legal nor a political decision. Could you explain whether the attempt on

President Reagan's life led to a review of legal guidelines concerning presidential disability, and what advice may have been given to those in the White House?

MR. FIELDING: At the time of the Wilson situation, of course, the Twenty-fifth Amendment did not exist. When President Reagan was shot on 30 March 1981, the new government had just begun to function, and it is interesting to note how well it did operate on 30 and 31 March, if one considers that the White House Situation Room that day was filled with a new Cabinet and White House staff who were basically strangers to each other. They had only been working together since 20 January, at best.

My office at that time had started to compile a book dealing with presidential disability, but on 30 March the book wasn't yet finished. What we did was to review the law. No decision was made to exercise the Twenty-fifth Amendment at that time. There was a great deal of communication, however, with Vice President Bush, who was then out of town.

One of the most interesting periods of my years in the administration occurred when the President had his cancer operation (13 July 1985) several years later during which, for the first time, the Twenty-fifth Amendment was exercised. It was interesting because no rule book is given to presidents explaining how to handle particular situations. There was great reluctance on the part of President Reagan to be the first one to exercise the Twenty-fifth Amendment because he realized that whatever he did would set a precedent. A great deal of reluctance to exercise the Twenty-fifth Amendment had always existed. The argument was that if the president is going to have his tooth filled, he can either bite a silver bullet and not go under the anesthesiologist's fine hands, or he can exercise the Twenty-fifth Amendment. Suddenly, then, the vice president becomes president until the president gets out of the dental chair. On the other hand, there is the question of what to do in the case of a lingering illness. It is quite a debate.

As the documents show, President Reagan said that he would transfer his power, but that he did not want to set a precedent. His concern led to a compromise between simply exercising the Twenty-fifth Amendment on the one hand and not exercising it on the other hand. Still, now that someone has jumped into the pool, it will be much easier for a future president to exercise the amendment. A more difficult situation would occur if the president was not able to exercise it himself, meaning that if he did not anticipate an illness or an operation, for example. Everyone's favorite spy novels will come into play as they think about the possibilities that could occur there. Fortunately, the United States has never been faced with that situation.

The Miller Center should be proud to know that immediately after the new administration took office, or perhaps even before Inauguration Day, there was an intense meeting, which I was peripherally involved in, at which the Miller Center report on presidential disability and the Twenty-fifth Amendment was reviewed. Additionally, President Bush and Vice President Quayle held a meeting dealing with the issue between the two of them.

QUESTION: Several of the conflict-of-interest issues that arose during the Reagan administration turned into major political issues for CIA director William Casey and White House counselor (later attorney general) Edwin Meese. In other cases, trials took place. How would you evaluate the way those issues were handled by the press and the Congress once they became major public concerns?

MR. FIELDING: It is hard to give you a broad answer because Deputy Chief of Staff Michael Deaver's situation, for instance, was very different from Ray Donovan's and the discussion surrounding Bill Casey's financial holdings. The problem, however, harks back to what I said before about the growing tendency to criminalize political debate. If someone fills out a form incorrectly, it seems to generate an assumption or presumption of venality instead of stupidity or inadvertence.

Although many mistakes were made in the reporting in the Meese situation, from a legal point of view it did highlight the problems that existed with the reporting requirements. The image created with the aid of the media was that someone who served as counselor and attorney general to the president was somehow evil. Neither that, nor the revised regulations, necessarily contributed to good government, but those are technical aspects that have not yet been worked out. People in the United States still live in an era where the media takes such matters to the point of public tolerance and sometimes beyond it.

NARRATOR: I once worked in an organization whose president had an extremely magnetic quality about him. When you were interviewed for a job by this particular president, he made you feel as though nothing else in the world could be as important as what you were going to do or were doing for him. Or if you had received another offer and went to tell the president about it, it was common to leave that office feeling shamefaced that you had even bothered him. Did President Reagan exhibit a similar magnetic quality when you talked to him?

MR. FIELDING: I have already confessed that he "rolled" me into taking my job. As a matter of fact, after he had told me not to worry about not being able to give him a four-year commitment, and I had said that I would do it, he paused and said that he had been putting off our talk all day because everyone had told him it would be the hardest sell he would have to make. I responded by saying that I didn't want him to think his new lawyer was a pushover, but that if I went home and thought about it, I probably wouldn't accept. His charm was therefore a factor. I have the greatest respect for the office of the presidency, regardless of who is holding it. I also have great respect for anyone who is deemed by the American people to hold that office, but in addition, President Reagan himself had a great deal of charm.

The other thing about Ronald Reagan was that if someone wished to leave the administration, he might persuade that person not to leave at a particular time. If the person personalized the reason he or she were leaving, however, that would be the end of it. From my experience and the experiences of others I know, he would respect those wishes. He would not make a person feel as though he or she were letting him down. He would be grateful that the person had been willing to serve in his administration, but he would never hold people beyond a reasonable time. Of course, one was still afraid to go in and ask him.

NARRATOR: Did you change your mind about Reagan during the period of your service? Did your original evaluation of him change in terms of qualities you might not have seen in the beginning?

MR. FIELDING: My original evaluation of him was one of great respect, but it was not complete because I came to hold even greater respect for him, his leadership, and his uncanny sense of what was right for the American people at the time, as well as for his sense of the American people's level of tolerance and acceptance of tough decisions. He had an uncanny instinct in that regard. Of course, he was also very charming in dealing with people, and although he had a temper like everyone else, he did not show it publicly very often.

One strange vignette that I witnessed involved a call I received from then director of the FBI, William Webster. Apparently, the operators of an abortion clinic had been kidnapped by a group calling itself the Messengers of God, or something like that, and the clinic's operators were to be killed unless the President did certain things. One of the things this group wanted the President to do was go on nationwide television and make a speech about the evils of abortion.

I told the President about it first thing in the morning. Someone in that arena knows instinctively and intuitively what he must do, yet his immediate instinct was that if anything could be done to prevent the group from killing those people, he had to do it. The debate went on for several hours. The President didn't need me to tell him that if he went on television that time, he might as well reserve 15 minutes every morning to placate whatever group wanted to be placated. Although he knew what leadership was all about, there was still that human element to his personality as well.

QUESTION: Do any guidelines exist concerning government documents that apply when a person leaves office? When Secretary of State Kissinger left, and even before he left, many of his materials were transferred to Governor Nelson Rockefeller's estate. Does any requirement mandate that such documents remain in the custody of the federal government so that they don't end up all over the country?

MR. FIELDING: As an aside, White House records are kind of an anomaly. A department or an agency will have records and records of records. If someone wants to know what the wheat quota was in 1850, a record for that would be available. When a new administration comes in, however, the White House file drawers are totally empty. Nothing is left because all documents are taken to a presidential library or repository.

In answer to your question, documents that are generated now should not be removed. They are property of the United States government. I know the incident you are talking about, but I don't think I'll comment any further.

QUESTION: The problems of ethics in government hit the Department of Defense at a very high level. How did someone like Paul Thayer (nominee for deputy secretary of defense) get to the level he did without being checked earlier in the process?

MR. FIELDING: The Paul Thayer situation was shocking to me. His FBI report went through my office. It had been screened by very fine professionals as well as my staff people. We had created a security office that did all of the pre-screening, and each file was then reviewed by at least one of my attorneys. After that point, if there were a problem, it would be reviewed by me personally. I also reviewed all Cabinet and deputy-Cabinet levels in addition to these cases.

When the Paul Thayer situation broke, I went back and pulled everything together that I had, and I went over and over it. Some of the people who had been involved with him criminally had been interviewed by the FBI. I agonized over this situation until I realized that he had been involved in insider trading. People that are involved in insider trading don't talk to the FBI about it when they are being interviewed. That was basically the problem.

What didn't show up—and I guess there is only so much one can uncover—was that the man had led a double personal life, aside from the insider trading. Some people from each life were interviewed, but we didn't realize that he was leading a double life.

QUESTION: You were involved in one of the most highly politicized administrations in the history of the United States. To what degree did your office and Mr. Reagan regard legal issues as subordinate to political concerns? When the administration was faced with the Boland Amendment, was it faced not with a legal but a political issue, which merits not a legal but a political response?

MR. FIELDING: There is a political element to everything done in the White House, and as a lawyer, it is just another element with which one has to deal when representing any client. It is a fact of life, and it is a consideration.

The Boland Amendment, as far as I recall, is an amendment that the administration did not like, but one that it was aware of and which it knew must be observed. I'm glad I said earlier that I left when I did, but to my knowledge, the Boland Amendment was being observed. Everyone was aware of it and the limitations it imposed.

As for your question about subordinating legal issues to political expediency, I never observed such a thing, and I was involved in much of the judicial selection. For instance, where it was very easy to put political before quality considerations, it did not happen, I'm happy to say. It would have been a very difficult situation for me if it had happened.

The fact that President Reagan enabled the White House counsel's office during the years that I was there to really institutionalize the counsel's office speaks to that question as well. There was an institutionalization of the White House counsel's office within the White House staff, even though there is no statutory basis for establishing a White House staff with a chief of staff or a counsel to the president or any particular office. The White House staff, as far as appropriations go, is a dollar figure, and a president is entitled to appoint X or Y number of people at X or Y rate. That is all the law requires.

QUESTION: You mentioned the War Powers Act. What is your view on how to circumvent it legally so that the country's chief executive officer can exercise his commander-in-chief role?

MR. FIELDING: Presidents have always acknowledged that the act exists, but they usually say that it is not applicable to their instant situation. From my experience, the biggest difficulty with the War Powers Act is that it has not been reviewed by both branches at a time when it is not an issue. Instead, both branches have generally reached a point where they know they have a problem, and then they start debating the nuances of the War Powers resolution. Congress needs to take a step back when the act is not an issue and look at what it wants to accomplish, what is practical, and what the difficulties are.

NARRATOR: What was the President's attitude toward law in relation to politics? I knew a chairman of a board of trustees who once said that if a lawyer gave advice that one did not want to follow, one should get a new lawyer. That was his attitude toward the law.

MR. FIELDING: I don't mean to repeat or be glib about my answer, but from my conversations with the President and based on the fact that I was included in so many of the administration's decisions, my opinion is that President Reagan felt legal issues were quite important. Moreover, not only the President, but also the chiefs of staff and others included me in decisions. The legal element was one that they wanted to be considered.

At the same time, however, there are instances in which legal issues can be viewed apart from political issues and cause a great deal of trouble. For example, many people have had discussions about Cabinet government and why there is not pure Cabinet government, but the Reagan administration was close to a pure Cabinet government due to the Cabinet committees and councils.

That situation was illustrated and reinforced by the creation of Cabinet councils in conjunction with the incident that occurred with the tax exemption for Bob Jones University. A seminar could be held on what happened in the Bob Jones case in 1985, but it essentially boiled down to the fact that many people were looking at the issue purely from a legal perspective and ignoring the politics of the matter. Both factors have to be considered when looking at an issue.

NARRATOR: Could you also explain the judicial selection process? Would you be willing to talk for a moment about any of the Supreme Court choices with which you might or might not have been involved?

MR. FIELDING: Let me talk about the Reagan administration judicial selection, because when I was in the Nixon White House, judicial selection was something that was handled between the attorney general or the deputy attorney general and the president, the chief of staff, or the head of domestic policy. There wasn't much screening or input from the White House. The choices were made basically at those higher echelons of government.

In the Reagan White House, we early on created a judicial selection committee to review the process. First, we recommended to the President that he do away with the executive order President Carter had issued, which created judicial selection commissions around the country for the various circuits. From our review, we determined that this process didn't remove the politics from judicial selection. It simply placed responsibility one step away. Thus, the process created a worse situation, in our view.

We also created a judicial selection commission within the White House, which was chaired by the counsel to the President. The members of the committee were the attorney general, the deputy attorney general, the assistant attorney general for legal policy, and occasionally, another assistant attorney general. The chief of staff was also a member, as were several of the President's assistants.

The tentative selection of those we were going to recommend to the President for a vacancy was made at that committee meeting, which brought the process into the White House, per se. This change basically resulted from the President's expressed desire to be directly involved in the judicial selection process. He wanted to ensure as best he could that judges he appointed had a judicial philosophy consistent with his mandate. President Reagan had a great deal of experience in this regard because as governor of California he had appointed many judges. The President and those who had elected him were very disappointed in the California selection process experience, and he vowed that he was not going to let that happen in his White House.

NARRATOR: Did the Douglas Ginsburg case result from a slip by the FBI or a slip in the organized process?

MR. FIELDING: I must be the luckiest man in the world because I was gone by then. The Ginsburg case involved his use of marijuana, but it is interesting how quickly things change and how quickly there has been a recognition that we live in an era where many of the very finest people have experimented with marijuana as youths. It may still be the same evil, but it has become a more universal evil and something that we have had to deal with. Usually a change like that occurs over 20 years or so instead of a span of just a few years.

QUESTION: Did you feel as though you were operating in a paranoid atmosphere during your eight years in the Nixon administration?

MR. FIELDING: I didn't have time to be paranoid because everyone was constantly attacking me! The last couple of years of the Nixon White House were—I don't know if paranoid is the right word—a terrifying and confusing period for those of us on the staff. If anyone can, imagine a situation in which the highest ranking people in one's organization are suddenly being accused of doing *X, Y,* and *Z*—accused of horrible things and being dismissed. One did not know what had really occurred, why it had occurred, or what the President knew and when he knew it. There was also the constant barrage of press, as well as the investigations.

I was deputy to John Dean for a period of time, then deputy to Leonard Garment, and after that, deputy to Fred Buzhardt. Having been John Dean's deputy, I was interviewed by many different entities, organizations, subcommittees, and subgroups—easily over 30 or 40 in number. It was hard to get my day's work done when I was trying to remember what someone said to me three years ago! So again, I didn't have time to be paranoid. It was a very unpleasant and, to a certain extent, disillusioning period.

In defense of the Nixon White House, however, it would be very interesting to look at an interoffice phone directory that I recently found, which was dated within about a week either side of the Watergate break-in and includes the names of those in the White House complex at that time. So many people who are now in government and who have contributed tremendously to government for the past 20 years were in the Nixon White House. Dick Cheney, for instance, was on the Nixon White House staff, along with a multitude of others. The staff was a very good and very poised staff, but Watergate inundated everyone and every agenda.

NARRATOR: You were general counsel to the second inaugural committee, as I understand it, and you will probably be the only person involved in our Reagan oral history who is likely to tell us much about either inauguration. The press covered the first one with great ferocity, and I wonder if there is anything that we ought to include in our history on inaugurations.

MR. FIELDING: An inauguration would be an interesting study. It involves assembling a huge organization in late November, raising millions and millions of dollars, having all kinds of events, and then dismantling that organization on 20 or 21 January. It would be interesting to look at the coordination between the political side of a party and the government itself. It requires much care. One has to worry not just about the contract with the caterer but also about how to pay the military units, for example. Everyone loves a parade, but no one wants to pay for it. How will the units get there? How will one deal with the taxpayer-dollar issue? In our inaugural situation, the foundation actually had some money left, but nonetheless, the situation generally involves lots of problems.

NARRATOR: Fred Fielding remains one of the best educators the Miller Center has ever had on the actual process of presidential leadership and presidential organization, and we are grateful to him.

CHAPTER 2

THE REAGAN PRESIDENCY:
A CHIEF OF STAFF'S PERSPECTIVE*

KENNETH M. DUBERSTEIN

NARRATOR: Kenneth M. Duberstein is chairman and CEO of The Duberstein Group, an independent, bipartisan planning and consulting company that provides strategic advice, counsel, and assistance on national and worldwide political, economic, and social developments. He succeeded Howard Baker as chief of staff for President Reagan in 1988. Earlier, he had been deputy chief of staff and has a long history of working with Senator Baker. Mr. Duberstein was also deputy assistant to the president for legislative affairs at the beginning of the Reagan administration and then assistant to the president for legislative affairs in from 1982 to 1983. He had a prominent role in building the coalitions on which major legislation of the Reagan administration was based. In the Bush administration, he coordinated on a pro-bono basis the confirmations of both Bush Supreme Court nominees.

In the Ford administration Mr. Duberstein was deputy undersecretary of labor, and during the Nixon administration he served as director of Congressional and Intergovernmental Affairs for the U.S. Government Service Administration (GSA). Prior to his directorship, he served as administrative assistant to the president of Franklin and Marshall College.

Presented in a Forum at the Miller Center of Public Affairs on 19 May 1994.

He was awarded the President's Citizens Medal by President Reagan. He has held several administrative leadership positions in the private sector, including vice president of Timmons and Company, a Washington government relations firm. Mr. Duberstein is a member of a number of boards of directors: McDonnell Douglas Corporation, Cinergy, the American Stock Exchange, the Kennedy Center for the Performing Arts, Ford's Theater, the American Council on Capital Formation, and the Bryce Harlow Foundation.

Mr. Duberstein will be discussing how a successful coalition can be built when boll weevils, Republican loyalists, and other elements are involved, and why coalitions are necessary even in a landslide presidential election victory.

MR. DUBERSTEIN: My focus today will be on my first-term responsibilities and my return to the White House in early 1987 as deputy chief of staff with Howard Baker, hoping to ensure that the last two years of the Reagan presidency would not be in vain. In my view, they were especially good years, not only for the country economically, but for the world and arms reductions.

I was not involved in the Reagan campaign of 1980. In fact, I was enjoying my life outside of government after having served in the Nixon and Ford administrations. Therefore, when the transition team asked me to consider returning to government as the President's chief liaison for the U.S. House of Representatives, initially I was reluctant. Although the Republicans had gained control of the Senate for the first time in 25 years with Howard Baker as majority leader, the House was still ruled by Tip O'Neill, Jim Wright, and the liberal Democratic leadership. I viewed a position as the President's top representative in the House a great opportunity. Even though the Reagan administration was likely to be successful in a Republican Senate, if it did not succeed in the House as well, the Reagan presidency would be off to a rocky start. Because I knew many of the House Republicans and House Democrats, I accepted the job with President-elect Reagan.

I visited a crusty old Democratic congressman (who is still in Congress) who had been in Washington long enough to have seen presidents come and go. I told him I was about to embark on this position for President-elect Reagan and asked for his advice on how to help Reagan make a difference and also serve the country, the

President, and Congress. This congressman chewed on his cigar, looked me in the face, and said, "Duberstein, you are smarter than 95 percent of the people here. You know it, and I know it. But what you have to remember is we're elected and you ain't!" That advice served me well during my tours of duty at the White House and subsequently.

To win in the House of Representatives, 218 votes are needed; yet in 1981 Republicans controlled only 191 seats in the House. Parenthetically, I wish that once in my lifetime I had 257 Republicans on my side of the aisle and that I could afford to lose 40 votes and still win, as President Clinton has had the luxury of doing. Even though Republicans held 191 seats, they were not necessarily going to vote unanimously for everything Ronald Reagan wanted. The Reagan administration had to reach out to the so-called conservative Democrats, referred to previously as boll weevils, from the Southern conservative districts where Reagan had run strongly in the 1980 campaign. Unlike Bill Clinton, Reagan finished ahead of almost every member of Congress in his or her district in the 1980 election. As a result, members thought either they could be reelected on Reagan's coattails or that Reagan was such a big force in their district that they could not disregard what he wanted.

During the transition I consulted Thomas G. Loeffler, a House Republican from Texas, who had previously served in the Ford administration in Congressional Relations. I asked him to introduce me to some of the boll-weevil Democrats. On a snowy December morning, I met with Loeffler and Texas congressman Charles W. Stenholm. Charlie Stenholm had been estranged from the Carter administration. He was horrified with the high interest rates, the high unemployment, the low respect for the United States around the world, and the loss of self-confidence here at home. We began to get acquainted and tried to determine the areas in which we could work to form coalitions that would reduce spending, increase U.S. national security, and cut taxes. Stenholm said that he was not an out-front leader but would try to ensure that I met all of the boll weevils. He proposed beginning with work on spending cuts to restrain federal spending. The meetings began in December 1980, about a month before President Reagan was sworn in.

During those tough times under a Democratic president, the United States had lost confidence as a nation, and with the economy spinning out of control, Reagan provided hope. The hostage situation in Iran and the loss of confidence in the United States throughout the world contributed to this situation. The Carter administration was winding down and had a horrendous relationship with Congress. They had begun badly and never recovered.

On 20 January 1981, when President Reagan was inaugurated and I began working at the White House, one of the first things I told my staff was that we were going to visit all 435 House offices. I said we would try to meet all members of Congress, and if they were not available, we would at least introduce ourselves to those members' staffs. My staff thought I was "crazy." I pushed for these visits because I wanted to demonstrate a distinct departure from the Carter Congressional Relations operation. We were new, and we wanted to have a good relationship with Republicans and Democrats alike. We knew that any coalition would not be fixed, but would be one that shifted like the sand on every vote. Moreover, even if the most liberal Democrat would never give his or her vote, he or she still might provide information that could then be used to garner the necessary 218 votes.

I personally met with all of the Democratic committee chairmen as part of this process. One of the committee chairmen showed me two letters. The first one, dated 21 January 1977, was from the head of Congressional Relations in the Carter White House and said how much he looked forward to working closely with this congressman. The last letter was dated 19 January 1981. It said, "I have enjoyed the privilege of working closely with you." The congressman looked at me and said that he never saw that person between those dates. He added, "I may never vote for anything that Ronald Reagan wants, but I will try to help you out procedurally, and I hope you will listen to what I want." He was right; he never voted for anything Ronald Reagan wanted, but he did help out on procedural votes.

The story of our visit with him spread, and other similar stories circulated, showing that this guy from California, who was best known as an actor, was taking Washington seriously and was trying to engage not only the Republicans, but the Democrats, in a dialogue to get his program going. We sent the message that the White House was an open door and would work with liberals, moderates, and conservatives. Interestingly, one other reason for making these visits was to obtain information: Who were some of the Democrats who might be willing to vote for what Ronald Reagan wanted in his economic package? What would a staff person tell our staff? What could we find special about their district? By what percentage did Reagan carry their district in 1980? For example, when a member of my staff visited a Democratic congressman's office, the congressman wasn't in, so he introduced himself to his staff. The congressman's top assistant told this staffer that Ronald Reagan carried this congressman's district by over 60 percent and that his congressman really wanted to help Reagan on his economic package. In Washington, when someone says they really want to help a person, it means almost nothing. It certainly does not mean one has a vote; still, the door is at least open.

Months later, during President Reagan's recuperation following the assassination attempt on his life, Reagan's staff members lobbied hard for the Reagan presidency's first major piece of legislation, the Gramm-Latta I budget. It was the first budget resolution of Ronald Reagan that reduced the level of spending increases. The press focused on the fact that the administration was trying to build a coalition of Republicans and so-called boll weevils. The networks, the *Washington Post* and the *New York Times* reported that Reagan had been unable to break into the Northeast or the Midwestern Democrats. In their view, he was simply trying to persuade the conservatives. Although they might be enough to succeed, the strategy did not reflect any broad scale support in the Northeast and Midwest. In light of this criticism, the administration began looking for support among Northeastern and Midwestern Democrats. One possibility was the Democrat from Pennsylvania whose administrative assistant my staff member had talked to earlier. I called the congressman, and he indicated that he would try to be helpful. Although he would not be prepared to make any commitment, he said that he would continue to pray on it and think about it.

Ronald Reagan, as part of his recuperation, began to call congressmen from the upstairs residence of the White House to ask for their support. I took a chance and recommended that President Reagan call this Democratic congressman from Pennsylvania. The White House switchboard tracked him down, and he was in the middle of a live radio call-in show, back home in Pennsylvania. The next voice heard was the voice of Ronald Reagan asking him for his vote. The congressman became flustered, and he committed. He said yes. Talk about the luck of the Irish. This was the first time the American people had heard Ronald Reagan's voice after the assassination attempt, thereby guaranteeing that the tape of this congressman committing to vote for the Gramm-Latta I budget played on all three networks and CNN that night. This congressman had no room to retreat. Ronald Reagan then broke into the Northeast and Midwest, ultimately winning votes from 63 Democrats and every House Republican.

In those initial weeks as the Reagan staff demonstrated that it wanted to be open, fair, and helpful to Republicans and Democrats alike, many meetings were held in the White House with the Cabinet agencies and the Office of Management and Budget (OMB) in an attempt to formulate that first budget resolution. The meetings focused on a large number of cuts, although in hindsight, perhaps not enough. They focused on trying to make required spending cuts wherever possible to begin reducing the deficit and to improve the economy. We spent time not only with the boll weevils, but also with some of the moderate Republicans, who did not completely support spending reductions or who had other spending priorities. The administration was concerned about losing any Republicans and about opening more channels to the conservative Democrats. I continued to promise the boll-weevil Democrats that they would be pleased with the President's proposal. Meetings, not just announcements, were conducted to negotiate yet more spending reductions.

On the night of 18 February 1981, Ronald Reagan gave his first major speech as President before a joint session of Congress to present his economic recovery package. That night, as the President departed the House chamber, I ran into Charles Stenholm. I asked him and some of his colleagues if Reagan had fulfilled what I had promised them. Charlie looked at me and said, "No, Reagan was a bit stingy." Stenholm thought Reagan could have found another $10 billion in spending cuts. I knew at that moment that the administration was close and could win that first budget resolution. If the Reagan administration hadn't cut enough to please the conservative Democrats, they would help find additional cuts, and certainly what had been recommended would be acceptable.

More than 50 members, predominantly boll weevils, were invited to have breakfast with Ronald Reagan the morning after his speech to discuss further spending cuts. We had met with the Republicans shortly before the speech and wanted to consult with the Democrats to bring them into the process before the formal legislation was submitted. It was that spirit of trust with both sides agreeing that the administration would address their concerns that helped Reagan build a successful coalition of Democrats and Republicans.

Ronald Reagan used the powers of the White House, known as the "bully pulpit," better than any president since FDR. He spoke to the American people and explained things to them. He brought them in on the takeoff, not just the landing. The staff initially viewed negatively Reagan's Saturday morning radio program on which he always spoke for five minutes. Reagan believed, however, that it gave him a chance to talk to the American people without any filtering by the press. He spent a great deal of time thinking about what he wanted to share with the American people for those five minutes. He also knew that his comments would make headlines on Saturday afternoon and evening on television and that they would guarantee some prominent television and newspaper coverage on Sunday morning, allowing him to dominate the weekends with his message.

Reagan also campaigned throughout the country. Those Democrats who opposed Reagan did not want him to visit their districts because they did not want the President to incite the people into sending letters and making phone calls to Washington. The administration had a popular weapon, and the President realized that he could apply pressure simply by appearing in someone's district. Those districts were chosen carefully, of course.

Reagan also understood that to be an effective legislative president he needed to be both revered and feared, not only throughout the world, but certainly in the United States. In 1980, with regard to the Carter presidency, people questioned whether the office had too many responsibilities for any one person. They stopped doubting when Ronald Reagan was president.

Many politicians were afraid to have Ronald Reagan visit their districts. Many said that they would prefer he stay out because his visit would make it more difficult for that congressperson. Those people did not like the fact that Reagan ran ahead of them in their

districts and therefore did not want him there. Sometimes the
Reagan staff asked Reagan to go to certain districts and apply
pressure because if Reagan could win that congressman's support,
it would open up other opportunities. The administration thus
played the strategy of reverence and fear.

The Carter administration had too many priorities. Everything
was a priority, and therefore nothing was a priority. If an
administration focuses attention on one or two issues, it will
communicate well with Congress and the American people. If the
message is constantly communicated, it will usually receive media
coverage. If the administration instead reacted to other people's
agendas, it would be playing another's game, not its own. During
the first months of his presidency, Ronald Reagan spoke only of
stimulating the economy by reducing spending, reducing taxes,
reducing overburdensome regulation, and increasing national
security. In fact, all of the votes in that first year were related to
the economic package, with the exception of one major vote on the
Saudi Airborne Warning and Control System (AWACS) that
required Senate ratification. Wherever Reagan went, he talked
about his Economic Recovery Program. As a result, members of
Congress couldn't say that they wanted to help the President but
would help him on a transportation matter because that was what
really mattered to Reagan. What mattered to Reagan was implementing his economic package. He communicated often to the
American people that it was important to them for his package to
be passed. The staff deleted matters from his schedule unless they
fit into the Economic Recovery Package campaign. By concen-
trating consistently on his message and by finding new ways to get
the story covered, Reagan was assured of success; the administration forced everyone to play its game.

Admittedly, the Reagan administration made plenty of
mistakes. During his recuperation from the assassination attempt
I once asked President Reagan to phone a particular congressman
who happened to be a "boll weevil." I had not done my staff work
well, and I didn't realize that this congressman was in Australia with
a congressional delegation headed by Tip O'Neill. The White
House switchboard tracked him down, and as President Reagan told
me the next morning, the conversation went somewhat like this:
"Hello. Boy, you sound groggy. What time is it and where are
you?" The congressman replied that it was three o'clock in the

morning and he was in Australia. Reagan looked at me and said, "All I felt like saying was, 'this is Jimmy Carter, goodbye!'" Instead, he apologized profusely to the congressman and asked him to come to the White House when he returned to Washington because he wanted to discuss the first budget resolution. Imagine this congressman coming downstairs in his hotel for breakfast in Australia and telling Tip O'Neill that while he slept, Ronald Reagan was making phone calls to Australia.

The administration knew that it had a safety net, the United States Senate, where it did have the votes. Still, the more support it could acquire in the House, the easier it would be for Howard Baker and the Senate.

The ability to continue working with one's constituency yet convince the voters to understand and appreciate one's priorities is a hallmark of a strong president. Because he focused all his attention on the Economic Recovery Package, Reagan could not please the parts of his constituency that had other priorities. For example, social conservatives wanted to pursue their agenda on abortion, school prayer, and so forth. These good folks were not necessarily happy with the decisions to delay some initiatives, but Ronald Reagan insisted that economic recovery come first. It was the President—not Jim Baker, Ed Meese, or any others—who made the decision. At the time we believed that if the administration failed to win the necessary votes on the highly contentious social issues, the loss would diminish Reagan's stature. The fact that he was perceived as "king of the hill" gave him the ability to pursue some of those other initiatives later. Thus, all of the administration's efforts were focused on the Economic Recovery Package.

The White House staff was marshaled into the Legislative Strategy Group (better known as LSG) in which six people decided strategically where Reagan needed to go, especially legislatively; what the opposition was likely to do; and where Tip O'Neill would hit the administration. The staff charted a campaign in strategic and tactical terms. Accordingly, LSG arranged the President's schedule, deciding whether to recommend that Reagan give a speech, make a trip, do three days of interviews, or focus on a certain number of districts. LSG also strategized how the Democratic leadership was going to use the House rules to prevent bills from reaching the floor. That innovation continued for the first term but dropped off in the beginning of the second term. I reinstituted the LSG when I returned to the White House in 1987, and it lasted through the Bush presidency.

President Reagan was willing to meet with everyone whom LSG recommended—certainly on the Hill—if it was determined that the support of a person or group was necessary to build a winning coalition. He spent countless half-hour sessions with members of Congress, many of whom sat white-knuckled in the Oval Office. Ronald Reagan did not follow Lyndon Johnson's style as a heavy persuader. He instead used sweet reason, explaining why an initiative was important to the member's district and the difference his Economic Recovery Package would make back home with job creation, and so forth. Members would often respond by telling the President that they wanted to vote for him, but that they were not hearing anything from back home. Ronald Reagan then assigned other people the job of activating the so-called grass-roots. The administration had to find ways to reach people in the district and convince them to lobby their representative. The politicians wanted cover from back home, so Reagan would give a speech or an interview to a local paper, and phone calls would be made to generate the grass-roots work necessary for congressmen to feel comfortable about supporting an initiative in Washington.

It is often said that Ronald Reagan was a great communicator. He was also a great lobbyist. He was focused on the belief that he was elected to straighten out the economy, restore the United States' prestige around the world, and strengthen national security. He was very much an "outbox" president. He knew what he wanted to accomplish and kept his attention focused on those three or four major items. People like me were there to help him accomplish his major objectives and to take care of other business. I knew my boundaries, whether I was in charge of lobbying the House of Representatives or much later while serving as his chief of staff, and I knew what decisions I had to clear with Ronald Reagan.

It is often said that presidents tack back and forth. The key to tacking back and forth is being able to define early what victories are achievable. If presidents compromise at the end and it is perceived as giving in, they lose. A victory needs to be defined early in terms that are clearly understood so that presidents are perceived as gaining, not losing, strength by compromising. As Tip O'Neill once said, "What I hate most about making a deal with Ronald Reagan is that Reagan always gets 80 percent of what he wants." Reagan's philosophy was that he would take 80 percent every time and go back the next year for the additional 20 percent. If he had tried to win 100 percent, he would have been perceived as losing. That strategy may be too pragmatic for some, but Reagan used it wisely to govern effectively. Governing well, he used to say, is the best politics. Sound public policy results from firm principles that are well articulated and carefully constructed. One does not often get 100 percent of what he or she wants, but standing firm, being persistent, and trusting the people will move the ball down the field to victory. Keep at it, he used to remind everyone.

QUESTION: Some in the media, such as *Time, Newsweek, New York Post, New York Times*, and so forth, haven't been as kind toward the Reagan administration in the last three years as they were in previous years. They argue that the Reagan years weren't spending-and-tax cuts, they were simply spend and borrow. In their view, it wasn't so much Reagan leading Congress as it was Congress leading Reagan. How do you respond to this sort of criticism?

MR. DUBERSTEIN: In the last couple of years Reagan has taken some unfortunate hits, in part because people have short memories. Many members of the press don't remember the 1970s, with the gas lines, the double-digit inflation rate, a 20 percent prime rate, and high unemployment. They also don't remember the hostages in Iran.

Reagan fundamentally changed a great deal in this country. He made some mistakes, and clearly the deficit is a major problem. Nevertheless, he fundamentally made America first again. He made the country proud. He created 20 million new jobs and lowered unemployment to 5 percent. His presidency was marked by more than over 80 months of continued economic expansion—the longest economic expansion since World War II. Thus, he did many things right.

The last few years have been tough. George Bush's victory in 1988 was important because it continued in some ways the policies of the Reagan presidency. Beginning with the budget deal in 1990, the Republican party started losing its way, which has provided an opportunity for many people to criticize the 1980s as the decade of greed. Recently, it was discovered that someone made $100,000 on cattle futures in that decade while at the same time decrying greed. People can't have it both ways, so enough of the hypocrisy.

Reagan did a great deal for national security. His philosophy was simple: build up in order to build down. Reagan's idea was to rebuild the military and national security apparatus to convince the Soviets that, as he used to say, they weren't in this situation alone.

I accompanied Reagan to the Berlin Wall after my return to the White House in 1987, and I was with him at his summits with Gorbachev. We both knew, as did Gorbachev, who won: the American people and democracy. Ronald Reagan was largely responsible for tearing down walls so the Russian people could understand there was an alternative to committing all of their resources to national security.

QUESTION: How did your predecessors influence the way you worked, and what lessons did you learn from people such as Jim Baker or Don Regan? What mistakes did you try to avoid?

MR. DUBERSTEIN: I learned a great deal from Jim Baker. He is probably the best political manager I have ever seen. He was particularly good at taking Reagan's philosophy and using it to decide, with Reagan, how to define victory in ways that were achievable. He tried to help Reagan by running the White House staff as a partnership. Several people contributed at LSG and together functioned as a team. Baker was good with the press and Congress. He always told the staff that we would play on our turf, not on theirs. That approach helped me tremendously, not only later when I served as chief of staff but also in my daily relationships with President Reagan, Mrs. Reagan, the Cabinet, and others.

Don Regan was an unfortunate choice for chief of staff. He was a much better secretary of the treasury, a position for which he was well suited. But as chief of staff he forgot that as White House chief of staff he was still staff, not chief. The President was elected; he was not. Regan made the mistake of trying to do too much for Reagan and did not recognize that Reagan was *not* the retired chairman of the board. He was chairman of the board and CEO, and it was his presidency.

I also learned a great deal from Howard Baker. He was majority leader when I worked on the White House staff during

Reagan's first term. Howard Baker is the person who encouraged me to rejoin the White House staff early in 1987. I initially declined, believing that when one works for the White House once, it is an honor; when one does it twice, he is a glutton for punishment! After declining, I was summoned to the Oval Office to meet with President Reagan. I had been gone for about two-and-a-half years or so, but I had kept in contact with the Reagans in the interim. I walked into the Oval Office and Ronald Reagan stood up behind the desk, shook my hand, and said, "Howard told me all the reasons you can't come back. I just want you to know one thing. Nancy and I want you to come home for the last two years of the administration." I immediately agreed to return. When the President of the United States asks a person to be a part of his staff, one says yes.

Howard Baker conceived of this partnership where he and I would be co-equals and I would run things on a day-to-day basis. Howard taught me to be patient and focus on the essentials. He reinforced the fact that Reagan was president. Although he had been a rival of Reagan in the 1980 primaries and as Senate majority leader, he was always supportive of Reagan and believed in giving the best advice to Reagan, without any sugarcoating, always remembering that *Reagan* was president. Reagan was the person who made the final decision.

QUESTION: How do you view Clinton's coalition building and his prospects for health care reform?

MR. DUBERSTEIN: Clinton's efforts have been made easier by the fact that he has 257 Democrats in the House. He can afford to lose as many as 40 votes and still win; and he has done a pretty good job in losing 38, 39, or 40. As I said earlier, I wish that just once I could have had the opportunity to give away votes.

There is an art to campaigning and an art to governing. Clinton has yet to make the transition to governing. Governing requires bipartisanship from the beginning. With bipartisanship, a leader might not win everything he wants, but he wins a great deal of it. At times he says no to his ideological wing and yields a little bit. Clinton cannot have too many more battles in which he wins with only 218 or 219 votes or by the vice president breaking a tie in the Senate.

Health care reform is such a fundamental undertaking that neither political party wants to be held accountable for a result it cannot guarantee. Clinton will not find success in the area of health care if he continues his 218-vote strategy. After all, Pat Moynihan has said that health care in the House should pass with 250, 275, or 300 votes. That kind of coalition is necessary so that everyone understands he or she has some responsibility for the result. The Clinton White House has voiced support for bipartisanship, but on their terms; they have failed to conduct any kind of bipartisan negotiation, which would be helpful and correct. Interestingly, many people in Congress are beginning to talk among themselves in a much more bipartisan way regarding health care. I just wish that the White House would make some concessions and begin working with these people.

NARRATOR: Could you explain a bit further the chief-of-staff's role?

MR. DUBERSTEIN: As chief of staff, one must focus on bringing all of the loose ends together. For me, those worries involved fundamental decisions on arms control, the U.S. relationship with Gorbachev, and ratification of the INF Treaty. As chief of staff, I also traveled 25,000 miles across 16 states in an unprecedented fashion on the President's campaign for his incumbent vice president. When I returned to the White House in early 1987, many people viewed Reagan not only as a lame duck, but perhaps even as a "dead duck." It was thus Howard Baker's and my job to remind everyone that the administration still had two years in which it could accomplish a great deal, not only to change the world but to change the country. Other issues involving my role as chief of staff included dealing with questions concerning the President's agenda, including economic growth, and trade and welfare proposals, the last round of Cabinet appointments, and Supreme Court nominees. At the same time, Reagan's ratings in the polls continued to rise, contrary to most expectations. (Reagan left the presidency with a 68 percent approval rating, which is the highest rate for a two-term president at the end of his presidency since polling began in this century.) It was my job to construct a White House staff and to help focus the President's attention on two or three priorities where he could make a difference. Finally, I addressed issues related to the transition, which was essentially a friendly takeover. In short, it was my responsibility to manage Reagan's efforts to leave center stage at the right time.

QUESTION: Could you elaborate further on Nixon's advice to you concerning the Bush campaign?

MR. DUBERSTEIN: When it was clear that George Bush was going to be the nominee of the Republican party, I asked former President Richard Nixon if he would be willing to spend some time detailing what he thought an incumbent president should do for his incumbent vice president running to succeed him. I also asked if he could share any lessons he had learned from the Eisenhower years and the Eisenhower-Nixon relationship in 1960 that he thought would be particularly useful to President Reagan in trying to determine how and in what fashion he should campaign for then-Vice President Bush. I spent about an hour-and-a-half with him. He gave me chapter and verse of the 1960 campaign. One of the things he stressed was that the best thing Ronald Reagan could do for George Bush was to govern well.

Governing well meant keeping the economy strong, moving forward on arms control, and playing to Reagan's strengths. These accomplishments would all help George Bush. He told me it was important that Reagan not become a surrogate for Bush, but that he should be willing to campaign for him one or two days a week. He thought it was important that all of the White House staff keep in mind that Bush needed to be perceived as involved in every major decision so that the press could not write, "while Bush was out campaigning . . . ," and this strategy was the one that Reagan followed.

Nixon predicted that George Bush would ask me shortly before the election if Reagan could go to California because the only way George Bush could win California was if Reagan went there in the last few days of the campaign. I told Reagan what Nixon had said, and Reagan replied that the election would either be won or lost beforehand.

The week before Election Day, Bush's campaign manager, Jim Baker, called me and said, "We're within two points in California. The Vice President would like the President to go to California and do one more campaign stop. It makes the difference between

victory and defeat, and we want the President to go to California."
I walked into the Oval Office and told the President that Bush
wanted him to go to California. Reagan had that knowing smile
and asked me if I thought it would make a difference. I didn't
know the answer because I'm not a California expert. I excused
myself and told the President I wanted to talk with two people
whom I absolutely trusted in California politics. Both essentially
told me that Reagan could make a difference, but not in the areas
where Jim Baker wanted him to go; the part of California where
Reagan would have the most impact was in the south, not the north.
Reagan and I discussed the matter. He gave me instructions, and
I called Jim Baker and said, "Send Jerry Ford to the north. Reagan
will go to Orange County and San Diego. We will turn out our base
and Reagan will do it under those conditions."

The day before election day, we left at the crack of dawn for
California. We visited Long Beach and San Diego. The election
results from California in 1988 revealed that it was the turnout in
southern California that clinched the state for Bush, who won by
one-and-a-half or two points.

NARRATOR: We have thoroughly enjoyed having Ken Duberstein.
Thank you, Mr. Duberstein, for providing us with new insights and
a different perspective of the Reagan presidency.

CHAPTER 3

REAGAN AND THATCHER: A PERSPECTIVE FROM ABROAD*

GEOFFREY SMITH

NARRATOR: Geoffrey Smith needs no introduction and no lengthy statement as to his accomplishments and his career. He has lectured in this room and also in the Dome Room of the Rotunda. He is well known in American political science circles.

He has been most recently in residence at the Wilson Center in Washington, where he did a substantial part of the book on Thatcher and Reagan. That book has already been published in England. It will be published in the United States and in Japan.

Mr. Smith is in a sense the Hedrick Smith of Britain now. For many years he has written three 800-word columns a week on both national and international affairs. Now he has resigned from the *Times*, and the change has involved a new pattern of life, but he does continue to write in the *World Monitor* magazine of the *Christian Science Monitor* and other newspapers and magazines. His main task since his resignation from the *Times* has been writing books, and certainly as important as any topic one could choose is the relationship between Prime Minister Thatcher and President Reagan.

We are delighted that he could be with us. The opportunity to renew a personal acquaintance and to hear him is a rare privilege for the Miller Center.

Presented in a Forum at the Miller Center of Public Affairs on 1 April 1991.

MR. SMITH: It is a pleasure for me to be back here. I believe that the Reagan-Thatcher relationship was one of the most important episodes in the history of Anglo-American relations, because the personal relationship between the president and the prime minister is critical. I want to make the bald assertion that the relationship between Margaret Thatcher and Ronald Reagan was the closest there has been between a president and a prime minister in personal terms and ideologically. I am also aware that this is an ideal time to be speaking about Anglo-American relations. In the immediate aftermath of the Gulf War, the value of the relationship is particularly appreciated on both sides of the Atlantic.

I believe that neither country could have won the war without the other. The role of American military power goes without saying. But without British support I do not believe that the resolution to give approval for the war and authorizing the war would have been passed by the Senate. Without Margaret Thatcher in dialogue with President Bush—first at Aspen in the immediate aftermath of the Iraqi invasion of Kuwait, and then two days later at the White House, I don't believe the decisions would have been have taken quite so quickly.

Without Reagan and Thatcher—and this is where I see a continuum between the relationship between the two of them and what has followed after—I doubt that there would have been the same instinctive cooperation, the same assumption that at a point of crisis the natural thing to do was for the President of the United States and the prime minister of Britain immediately to get together.

George Bush was not actually at Aspen when the news of the invasion came through. Margaret Thatcher was. Quite understandably, members of his administration said to him when the news came through, "Well, Mr. President, you ought to stay here in Washington at a time of such crisis as this and cancel your visit to Aspen," to which Bush replied that at this time there was no more important thing that he could do than to talk with the prime minister. I doubt that there would have been that same assumption if it had not been for the pattern of relationship that had been developed between Reagan and Thatcher.

This has happened before. The creation of NATO in the late 1940s was essentially an Anglo-American operation. Since then other European countries have come to play a critical role in

NATO, but the actual formation was largely the work of the American and British governments.

Without the habit of cooperation established between our two countries during the Second World War, I think the creation of NATO would have been much more difficult. It wasn't only a habit of cooperation that was established in those years. The belief was restored on the British side that it was possible to influence American policy.

Some years ago an inferiority complex did develop on the British side. It was thought to be no use really trying to talk to the United States government because it was so powerful and we in Britain were so weak that it would have been a waste of time. That impression was corrected during the Reagan-Thatcher years.

It took a long time for this to sink in on our side of the Atlantic because there was a tendency in Britain to listen to the lavish public compliments that Reagan and Thatcher paid each other, to listen to Margaret Thatcher's remarks in public and to say, "There's the prime minister of Britain just ingratiating herself with the President of the United States." That kind of remark, which was heard and written quite a lot in Britain, certainly during the early years of the Reagan-Thatcher partnership, mistook the full dimension of the relationship.

First of all, there was the personal liking between the two of them. They got on well simply as individuals. The personal chemistry worked. As a number of his advisers mentioned to me, Reagan is a man who likes women and is comfortable in their presence.

Margaret Thatcher enjoys the company of charming, gracious, elegant, tall, handsome men. But she was not responding to the film star. When I saw her in connection with my book, she told me that she has never seen any of Reagan's films.

It was also important that they had an ideological affinity. They are both intensely ideological politicians, and they found that they shared the same ideology. If that had not been the case, the fact that Reagan liked her would not have been enough. He is a politician with a very strong sense of direction; he trusted those politicians whom he felt wanted to move in the same direction that he did.

Their first meeting was in April 1975, and they met again in 1978. In 1975 Margaret Thatcher had just been elected leader of the Conservative party. Ronald Reagan had just stepped down from being governor of California. The timing was important, because at that stage they were both in one sense in the wilderness—outsiders even in their own party. It was a year before Reagan challenged Ford, unsuccessfully, for the Republican nomination in 1976.

Margaret Thatcher, having just been elected the new leader of the Conservative party, still in a sense felt like an outsider. The other principal figures of the party hadn't really accepted her. "Thatcherism" as a political philosophy had not been accepted by British Conservatives. Only two members of her original shadow cabinet had actually voted for her to be leader. The two of them as outsiders always had the shared experience of being in the wilderness together. They were crusaders, still very much at the aspiring stage of their careers.

When they met again in 1978, this still applied. Neither of them was in power or could be certain that they were going to get power. But, in this crusading spirit, they seem to have discussed at those first two meetings a wide range of topics. Although both meetings lasted much longer than originally arranged, they were still jumping around from topic to topic. It must have been a discussion of broad generalizations.

What they found, in effect, was that they shared the same ideas, principles, and prejudices. When one of them hummed a tune, as it were, they found that the other knew the words. There was this sense of almost immediate accord between them.

There was much more to the relationship as it developed when they were in power than simply one of getting on well together because they were good friends sharing the same ideological instincts and objectives. Thatcher wanted to use the friendship to influence policy. She maneuvered and, when the opportunity presented itself, manipulated. In other words, she was concerned that while this was a friendship, it should not be just a friendship. It was certainly not going to be a cozy friendship, but a relationship of power and the determination of policy. It is these elements that give the relationship its historic significance.

Margaret Thatcher had the greater grasp of policy—not just details, but the general substance. While Reagan was a leader with a strong sense of direction, he left it to the people around him to transform his policy inclinations into programs. He would often leave it to his advisers and his Cabinet members—to "you fellas" as he would term them—to work out the specifics of his own policy ideas. Thatcher became in many respects during those years one of "you fellas"—one of those who had specific ideas, policy objectives.

They were not intellectual equals. Many people have said this to me, and not just British people. No one to whom I have spoken has said that they were intellectual equals. I must record this as a matter of history, as I spoke to most of the people who were most closely associated with both of them while I was doing the research for this book. Most of the people I have spoken to have quite specifically said the opposite.

I hasten to add that this does not mean, as I hope I will make clear, that she was just taking him by the hand. One of Reagan's advisers actually used that phrase to me and said that this was the impression that was given. That is not the assumption I am making. I am not suggesting that Reagan was an ineffectual leader. I am only suggesting that his gifts, which were powers of decision, powers of explanation, and the capacity to inspire friendship and trust, were qualities of a different nature.

Thatcher didn't realize this initially. Her first meeting came after Reagan was elected in 1980 and took office in January 1981; she was his first state visitor. This was quite deliberate on his part. He indicated as soon as he had been elected that he wanted this to happen. He was inaugurated in January 1981, and she came over in February of that same year.

In one sense that was an immensely successful visit. She was going through a bad time at home. She was not riding high in British politics. That affected quite a number of the people around Reagan who thought that they personally gave her a rapturous welcome when she came over in February 1981. When one goes back to the record, one finds it wasn't quite like that. Reagan gave her a rapturous reception at a time when many people over here were looking rather askance at her and thinking she was going to be another failed British prime minister.

In one respect her visit here was a disappointment to her, because she felt that there wasn't exactly the intellectual dialogue with Reagan that she had expected. On the two occasions they had met before in London they had gotten on famously, but had essentially been whistling the same marching tunes to each other. They had not really gotten to the detailed substance—the nitty-gritty of policy. In 1981 they were both in power. This was an opportunity to settle down around the table and say, "What are we going to do?" She found that Reagan didn't want that kind of discussion at all. She came out afterwards and remarked to one of her advisers, "There's nothing there! There's nothing there!", referring to the intellectual content.

In 1983 or 1984 the queen was in California on the royal yacht, and Reagan and his wife stayed with them overnight. The following morning Mike Deaver came up to Reagan with his speech for the day and explained one or two things about the speech—how you pronounce this name, how you pronounce that name. "Mr. President," he said, "this is your line on Nicaragua for today." One of the queen's advisers turned to her and said, "Well, ma'am, we'd never dare to give you a speech unseen like that for you to deliver in an hour or so." She replied, "Yes, and they call *me* a constitutional monarch!" This was a remark made only to her advisers, needless to say.

Reagan, in some respects, did give the impression of being the constitutional monarch, but the difference in intellectual grip of the detail of policy to some extent made up for the disparity in power between the two countries. I don't believe that the personal relationship would have worked quite the way it did if there hadn't been this extra contribution made by the British prime minister to compensate for the difference in national power. That was only possible because of Reagan's lack of vanity, which was to my mind one of the most extraordinary qualities displayed throughout this relationship, that someone who had reached a position of that sort should be so really modest in a personal sense.

In 1979, Thatcher had been elected prime minister, nearly two years before Reagan was elected to the White House. The first distinguished foreign politician to phone Thatcher with congratulations on her success was Ronald Reagan. The first time he phoned he was not put through to her. The call was taken by an aide in Downing Street who assumed that there were more important things for the newly elected British prime minister to do than to take a telephone call of congratulation from an ex-actor who had tried to run for President of the United States but had failed and clearly was not going to make it. But this rebuff did not put Reagan off. A couple of days later he phoned again and talked to her.

At the Williamsburg Economic Summit in 1983 at the opening dinner with just the heads of government present, Reagan in his opening remarks started to point to the old British colonial governors' portraits around the wall. His opening remark drew attention to them; he turned around to her and said, "Margaret, if one of your predecessors had been a little bit smarter"—at which point she jumped in, interrupting him and grabbing his punch line— "Yes," she said, "in that case, I would have been hosting this dinner—not you!"

What was striking to me when I saw Reagan was that he was the person who told me this story, and told with great relish how he had not been able to get his punch line out because she had come along and taken it. He told the story with immense pleasure and a sense of fun.

How much influence did the relationship actually have? I believe it mattered considerably. There were two categories of decision where it mattered. First of all—and I hope you will appreciate that I am picking out just one or two examples from many—let me take the question of the Falklands. There is a tendency nowadays, certainly on our side of the Atlantic, to underestimate both the amount of practical help that we received from the United States and the extent to which the American government was divided according to the conflicting pressures within it.

There were arguments until the end. Without Reagan's influence, without his decisions, American policy would not have been anything as helpful to Britain as in fact it was. I find it hard to believe that Britain would in fact have won in the Falklands without the practical assistance given by the United States with Ascension Island and in so many other ways.

It was not the case that Reagan took immense detailed specific interest in exactly what was happening. When I spoke to him recently, he mentioned , rather to my surprise, how it had lodged in his mind what a difficult issue this was for his administration because of the relationship with the whole of Latin America. But there is no question that he was the one who decided which way the United States government would come down. It was a difficult issue, but he decided that the United States was going to come down on Britain's side.

All the way through until the end, there was always, as I argue in my book, a public American policy and a private American policy. At no point did the two coincide. Initially the public American policy was to be evenhanded and try to draw both sides to an understanding so as to avoid war. That was the public American policy at that stage. The private American policy was to give Britain practical assistance. When the effort toward mediation had failed, then the public American policy was to support Britain; but the private American policy was still to keep up the pressure for mediation to try to get an agreement short of outright conflict.

This went on all the way through to the end. What was critical was that Reagan decided that Thatcher needed his support and that if the United States did not support Britain, the Thatcher government would fall and she would no longer be prime minister. He didn't, I believe, understand all of the ramifications or the subtleties of policy involved. While it was, as he put it to me, "a difficult decision for us," he nonetheless came down on our side when it came to the point. His relationship with Margaret Thatcher, I believe, was critical there.

Subsequently, there was the question of arms for Argentina. The American administration believed, not unreasonably, that with the change of government in Argentina, there was a case for selling some arms to the new regime—not arms that could be used for a further assault on the Falklands.

Thatcher was going to see Reagan at Camp David. The administration—Secretary of State George Shultz, Deputy National Security Adviser Colin Powell, National Security Adviser Frank Carlucci, and others—all worked on this issue. Position papers were developed and agreed on within the administration and sent to Reagan. They worked on it for some weeks with the aim of persuading Reagan to say to Margaret Thatcher, "Margaret, we are going to continue to support you, but we want to have friendly relations with the government of Argentina, which is now a democratic regime. We're just going to sell a few arms. Don't think that we're not being friendly to you." This was the idea.

The discussion went on at Camp David. The President didn't raise the issue; nothing was happening. Thatcher knew that this was going to come up, but the President never raised the matter, and the discussion continued. Then at the end, Thatcher opened her handbag, took out a list, looked up, and said, "Oh! Arms to

Argentina—you won't, will you?" Reagan said, "No, we won't." That was the end of it.

Some of Reagan's advisers were very displeased at the outcome of that discussion. They discussed what they should do. Should they raise it again? One of them said, "Raise it as much as you like with him, but I tell you, if you do, you'll just get rolled!" And that was the end of it. That is a remarkable example of just where the personal trust was dominant in terms of determining policy.

I would like to discuss briefly the extradition treaty and the question of whether citizens of Ireland who were suspected of aiding the IRA (Irish Republican Army) should be extradited from the United States for trial in the United Kingdom. I was told by Senator Richard Lugar (R-In.), who was then chairman of the Senate Foreign Relations Committee, that apart from the INF Treaty, this was the item of legislation for which Reagan lobbied hardest in Lugar's experience during his time as chairman of that committee. The night that the treaty was passed by the Senate, Reagan was on the phone talking to Margaret Thatcher with mutual congratulations, but saying in effect, "I've done it! I've delivered for you."

On the other side, there was the bombing of Libya. Speaking to Thatcher now, it is clear what a difficult decision it was for the British government to approve the use of American bases in Britain for the bombing raid on Libya. They agonized over it within the British government. But the decision that the American bases in Britain could be used for that raid depended critically on the relationship between Thatcher and Reagan. It was a personal decision by Thatcher. The issue was never brought before the British Cabinet until afterwards, and I have little doubt that if each individual member of the British cabinet had been consulted in a secret ballot as to whether they should support the use of the American bases or not, those American bases would not have been used. It's quite possible that if this had been discussed around the Cabinet table and Margaret Thatcher had been looking at each member of the Cabinet in the eye, they would not have summoned the nerve to say, "o, Prime Minister!" But if there had been a secret ballot of the British Cabinet, that would not have gone through.

Irangate is an interesting example where Thatcher knew about the arms deals nearly a year before they became public knowledge. She knew because the hotel room of Bud McFarlane in London was bugged. It was bugged within a few days of his stepping down as national security adviser in December 1985. Technically, there is the understanding, as we all know, that this doesn't happen between our respective governments. We don't bug you; you don't bug us. McFarlane was technically no longer a member of the United States government. But he came straight from a meeting at the White House to meet Ghorbanifar in London. He was on a mission on behalf of the President.

A couple of months later in February 1986, Antony Acland, subsequently the British ambassador in Washington, and Sir Percy Craddock, then the prime minister's foreign affairs adviser, came to Washington and saw Poindexter, who was then national security adviser. They raised the question with him: "Are you selling arms to Iran?" The answer that they received, I am told, was opaque. They decided that they knew well enough what was happening. They went back and reported this to a very small group of people in London, including Margaret Thatcher, and the decision was taken that this information was not-for-use, that they were not going to jeopardize the Anglo-American relationship. They were not going to jeopardize Thatcher's relationship with Reagan by raising this issue. They were just going to let the matter lie, which they did for over half a year before the whole Irangate episode became public knowledge.

This was significant, I believe, in two respects: first, because Margaret Thatcher decided that it was more important to preserve the relationship than to make a fuss about this; secondly, because she was assuming that despite the close relationship between the two of them, she would not have actually been able to change Reagan's mind. She must have been assuming that he knew about the arms deals. If she had come to the United States, gone to see Reagan at the White House, and said, "Ronnie, what on earth are you doing?" or even "What are your people doing?" that she would not haven't gotten anywhere. That was clearly the assumption she was making, because it was decided that this was not-for-use information.

Then there were the broad international issues. Gorbachev's first visit to London was in 1984, before he became leader of the

Soviet Union. He had something like a six-hour meeting with Margaret Thatcher, and she described that meeting to me, and I've described this in the book. It was after this meeting that she declared that he was a man she could do business with.

Then she came to Camp David and said to Reagan, "You know that you and I can talk together, that we can trust each other. I just talked to this new man from the Soviet Union. I'm telling you that you can talk to him, that you can have a dialogue with him." She did not exactly play the role of mediator, because she was careful not to be in a position of giving the impression of being evenhanded between the two of them. But while being Reagan's friend, Reagan's ally and partner, she nonetheless drew the two of them more into a dialogue.

Indeed, on the way over for his first visit to the United States, Gorbachev stopped at Air Base Bryce Norton in Britain, had lunch with Thatcher, and made clear to her in his remarks there that he saw this as a triangular exchange of views that had been taking place. The symbolism of stopping and of having lunch with Thatcher on the way to his first visit to the United States was itself of the greatest significance. I believe the development of the relationship between Gorbachev and Reagan and their role in ending the Cold War would not have taken place as it did without the friendship that Thatcher had established with Reagan, because she was thereby able to talk with all the greater confidence to Gorbachev.

From Gorbachev's point of view, she was of value as an interlocutor, which she would not have been without the friendship with Reagan. Because of the confidence she already had with Reagan, she was able to establish Reagan's confidence in developing the dialogue with Gorbachev.

I realize that you at the Miller Center are concerned with the study of the presidency. Thatcher also played the interagency game over here; she and others here knew when it would be beneficial to get a message to the President from her. The timing of messages to the President was frequently orchestrated by those over here who realized that they were her allies on particular policy issues. They would use this, and she would obviously know what was happening. The timing of messages would be synchronized with people in the administration here so that she was participating in the interagency battle that was taking place here. She was a player in the making of American policy.

I would like to offer two quick warnings before I finish. First, although I have said that I think she was the more dominant of the two in personal terms, she did not program him; she could not persuade him on those issues where his mind was firmly made up. When that was the case, she realized it and would back off.

There were two particular instances. One was on the budget deficit. At the Williamsburg Economic Summit, she used her bilateral meeting with him to try and persuade him about the budget deficit with the argument—"You believe in hard money; we both do." They didn't argue, but his eyes glazed over. When she came out, she knew that she had failed to persuade him. She said to her advisers, "I had a go at him; I talked all the time on this. I made no impression on him, and I'm not going to try and do it again." And she didn't.

Second, she never persuaded him to give up his aspiration for a nuclear-free world. He wanted to get rid of nuclear weapons. She never persuaded him that this was not the objective to go for; she could only persuade him that they could not actually take the next step here and now.

She described that objective to me in a previous interview as being "pie in the sky." I don't have the slightest doubt that this remained her view, and I don't have the slightest doubt that she failed to persuade him away from his objective.

Nonetheless, I believe that the history of the 1980s and the history of Reagan's foreign policy and much that happened subsequently in international affairs cannot be understood without an appreciation of the Reagan-Thatcher relationship. It was, I believe, the closest that there has been between a president and a prime minister of Britain. I believe it was a historic relationship and that indirectly it will continue to influence the future.

NARRATOR: One of our previous speakers got into some trouble for saying he didn't understand, at a certain point, President Reagan. I'll get into trouble for saying that I still don't understand one thing. You spoke so vividly the last time you were here about the system of rising in the Parliament and the exposure particularly to foreign policy issues for all of those who ultimately became prime ministers. They were prepared, in other words, for foreign policy as American politicians frequently are not. That would suggest that with that greater exposure, not only Mrs. Thatcher but some previous prime ministers would be tutor to a president in foreign policy.

The confusing part of coming to that conclusion is that in all of the media reports of the economic summits, particularly after the first year or two, one gets the picture of Reagan being the dominant figure in the economic summits, and Mrs. Thatcher playing sometimes a supporting role but not being the dominant figure. What would you say on that kind of an issue?

MR. SMITH: I think that this interpretation owes a lot to the public relation skills of Reagan's advisers. I believe that of the two of them at economic summits, nearly always she was the more dominant. She certainly spoke more, particularly in the first years when it really mattered.

She was the one who, in effect, spoke for both of them. The first summit they attended together was the Ottawa Summit of 1981. It was shortly after Reagan had been shot, and one doesn't know whether he had at that point really recovered his full strength.

But there is no question that then they were in a minority— probably a minority of two. That was at a time when Trudeau represented Canada; it was Helmut Schmidt, a Social Democrat, from Germany; it was Mitterrand, still in his strongly socialist phase when he was first elected president of France (at that time he wanted to pursue a much more socialist, left-wing policy than he has done subsequently).

The Japanese prime minister played no real part in dialogue; he would make formal statements, but play no real part in the argument. It was Thatcher and Reagan largely battling against the others. It was, I am told, the most abrasive of all of the economic summits that they had during their years together.

Thatcher was the spokesman for the two of them. At one point during the summit, Reagan was sitting with a yellow pad in front of him and had his pen. One adviser noticed that he had been sitting quite silently and writing. The adviser was rather interested to see what significant and telling remarks the President had been writing on his pad. He looked over his shoulder and saw a succession of heads with cowboy hats on them; that was all that was on the pad. Reagan was not so good at that kind of interchange with other heads of government. He became better later.

In general, he was the one who would tend to follow her lead on those occasions. Yet, there were some things that Reagan could do that were beyond Thatcher's range, as he demonstrated at the last meeting of NATO heads of government that he attended, when he was on his last swing through Europe before he retired. Each head of government had made a statement in turn, and then it was Reagan's turn. He got up to speak, and George Shultz pointed to his notes, which he was leaving behind, and Reagan responded, "I think I'll just take this on the wing, George," and George Shultz turned to his neighbor and indicated, in effect, that he did not know what they were in for now.

Reagan went to speak. I have spoken to a number of people who were there, including some British foreign office officials, and as many of you know, they can be pretty hard-boiled. One of them told me that it was one of the most memorable occasions in public affairs in his lifetime, hearing Reagan speak, totally without notes, about what the Western alliance and this friendship between nations meant to him.

One particular official, a senior British official to whom I have spoken about this, said to me, "Before then, I never realized what it was about Reagan that was so special. I had always thought he was rather a limited man who had gotten to very high office." Then he said, "I realize that this was something no other head of government there could possibly have done." It was the sincerity of the man that came across when he spoke then, quite simply, of what the Western relationship and this alliance of nations did mean.

QUESTION: Could one say there is grave risk in the personal summitry that goes back to the time of Roosevelt, Churchill, and Stalin—that we may come to an age where the heads of state may be pygmies instead of giants? In that case, might not the return to the institutional British Foreign Office and U.S. State Department talks and relationships prove much safer?

MR. SMITH: I take the force of this suggestion. I think in practice we will always find that it will oscillate; sometimes we will find that the regular lines of communication—the diplomatic officials on both sides—will be more influential in making policy, and sometimes they will be less influential. This will depend essentially upon the personality, political strength, and interests of the leaders concerned.

In general, I just do not believe that it is going to be possible—even if it were desirable—to go back to the age when foreign relations were essentially conducted by the established officials on both sides, when the formal lines of communication were the only ones that mattered.

I do not think it is going to be possible simply because of modern communications. The time has gone when heads of government do not meet and when they don't speak directly to the media in a way that is going to be seen and heard across the world. They are going to meet; they are going to be in direct communication.

There are some disadvantages in this. There is not the time for reflection, and there are occasions when heads of government get together, pick up the ball, and run with it, and people sit back and say, "What the devil are they doing?"

From the British standpoint, Reykjavík was one of those occasions. I have a phrase in my book that Thatcher used with me—I think the phrase was that it was the one occasion when she felt the ground was moving under her feet. She knew nothing about what was happening at Reykjavík until the last afternoon when a brief message was passed through to her. That referred only to a possible INF agreement. Yet they almost agreed on phasing out ballistic nuclear weapons. In Reagan's case, he was prepared to abolish nuclear weapons altogether. This was something she only knew about afterwards.

QUESTION: To what extent will this special arrangement that has been in place—and my own guess is that it will tend to continue at least in the immediate future—affect the position of Britain in the EEC; in effect, the partnership of the United States as it affects the relationship within the Community?

MR. SMITH: That is a very relevant point. I don't think it affects British membership in the Community.

If the Community were to develop to the point where there could only be a single foreign policy, and where Britain could not operate independently from the rest of the Community, it would clearly have a major effect on the British relationship with the

United States. This does not apply to the Community as it exists today. It does not affect Britain's role in the Community as of now. I do think it has a major influence on the way in which Britain would like to see the Community develop in the future.

If the Community had developed already to the point that there was a single European foreign and defense policy—and we know that there are demands for both of those developments within the Community—and if the Community had developed to the point where Britain could not operate independently, Britain would not have been able to play the role that it has in the Persian Gulf.

I referred at the beginning to Margaret Thatcher meeting George Bush at Aspen and the two of them getting together and talking, and then meeting a few days later in the White House. There they were talking about how they thought the West should respond. The West's response at that point was the United States' and Britain's response. Most countries of the European Community, with the exception of France, at that point were not keen on a strong response.

German public opinion was strongly against becoming involved, and we know that the German response has been essentially that of offering economic assistance. I am actually not particularly critical of the Germans here. I think one has to take into account the history of the last half century, and one has to take account of psychological attitudes in Germany today. But if you look around Western Europe, if we had been in the position of only being able to respond as a community or not at all, we would initially have done nothing, and ultimately there would have been a very limited response indeed. If we are going to maintain the Anglo-American relationship, there is a point beyond which we cannot go with European integration, because we have to retain the capacity of freedom of decision and freedom of activity for ourselves.

II

FUNCTIONS OF GOVERNANCE:
THE REAGAN PRESIDENCY

CHAPTER 4

THE GREAT COMMUNICATOR: THE REAGAN PRESIDENCY*

TOM GRISCOM

In his 38 brief years, Tom Griscom has had a remarkable political career, and he continued certain aspects of it as West Professor of Communication and Public Affairs at the University of Tennessee at Chattanooga. He was most recently assistant to the president for communication and planning, and in that position his thinking and planning drove the pattern of communication and discussions of the Moscow summit and President Reagan's personal diplomacy. Many of the speeches that President Reagan gave are memorable, notably, the Moscow State University speech. Tom Griscom had a major role in planning those speeches and editing and organizing them for delivery.

Tom Griscom began his career in Tennessee. He was a writer for the *Chattanooga New-Free Press*. At one time it was said that the Roundhouse, the arena in Chattanooga, should have been named after him because he generated such interest in its creation. He was affectionately called Scoop but also came close to being named for the state insect when a resolution was introduced in the state legislature to bestow that name on him. As press secretary to Senator Howard Baker, he was highly regarded on Capitol Hill, being called the best in his field. Howard Baker used to say that Tom Griscom's press conferences were better attended than his

---

Presented at a Lecture in the Dome Room of the Rotunda at the University of Virginia on 3 October 1988.

own, and when Senator Baker went to the White House, one of the first people to whom he turned was Tom Griscom. His subject is Reagan: Leadership and Communication.

MR. GRISCOM: I always find that it is probably best to begin a discussion by putting things in perspective, so let me first explain how I came to Washington and spent ten years of my life there. It is true that I was designated, if only for a few fleeting moments, as the state insect of Tennessee. I was beaten out by the ladybug beetle, and I guess that is appropriate, but I was the state insect for at least a short period of time.

I first arrived in Washington in 1978. I was at the *Free Press* at that point as a political writer, and Senator Baker was a candidate for reelection. He called me and said, "I need a press secretary. Would you come to work for me?" If you have ever been a newspaper reporter, particularly a political writer, the first thing you do is look through your clip file to find out what you wrote about him because you want to make sure that if you see him, he won't say, "Why did you say this about me a couple of weeks ago?" I looked through the file, and everything appeared to be OK, so I said I would like to take the job. He then asked me to come to Huntsville, Tennessee, a small town in the mountains about 60 miles west of Knoxville, to talk to him about the job. When I arrived, Senator Baker said, "I don't know why it took me so long to find you. I have looked now for six months. This search has taken me all across this country, and was someone right in my own back yard who could do the job." You can imagine the sort of swelling of pride I experienced, saying to myself, "My gosh, this is the minority leader of the United States Senate saying I'm the one person in this whole country who could do the job." I replied, "Senator, I'm really flattered you feel that way." He then said, "Let me tell you why. After traveling around, I cannot find anyone other than you who could see eye-to-eye on the issues with me." I thought for a minute and said to myself, "What he is telling me is that I am 5'6" now and I'd better not grow another half-inch." If you ever saw us traveling together, you always saw me standing next to Senator Baker, which made him look bigger and me smaller. That is how I ended up in Washington at the White House.

I would now like to present a broad review of President Reagan, his ability to communicate, and his use of communication to convey political ideas. I do not plan to deal in detail with specific incidents, although I will touch on them. Instead, I will focus on his ability to control the agenda through the use of communication. From my point of view, there are three basic elements of leadership. One is strength of character. Are the leaders strong individuals and can they display that strength? Second, do they have a purpose a direction for what they want to do? Third, can they through the first two elements exhibit at least some type of control and ability to dominate an agenda and become the person who can shape and give direction and form to public policy? These three points are critical in defining leadership. They are three elements that I think most presidents bring to the office. A particular president may not bring all three elements, but in the case of President Reagan, I think he did. This president was also probably best at taking what I see as a communication age that was developed by television and using it as a medium to deliver his message and deliver it in a dominant way. While he did not necessarily create all of the techniques used to communicate, he perfected some of them, expanded on them, and then used them to his own benefit.

President Reagan described himself as a leader with a new beginning, a new direction, and offering clear, concise goals for this country to follow. People say that he was simplistic because he wanted to talk about balancing the budget, cutting spending, cutting taxes, or rebuilding U.S. national defenses but that he could not sit down and deal with anyone who wanted to talk about the ins and outs of Superfund. Was that a strength or weakness from this President's standpoint? When he came into office, it was a strength for him because there was no doubt that this President understood who he was, the things he wanted to accomplish, and how to communicate those things to the American people. No one doubted that President Reagan was able to stand up and say, "This is what I believe, and this is the way I want to go," and then lead the country.

David Broder wrote the following about President Reagan's communication strategy in his book, *Behind the Front Page*:

> He was able to project his voice and his views more widely than any other politicians. It has enhanced the power of the communicator and chief as against that of other institutions of

government, particularly Congress and state and local officials. I would not strip any of these tools from the President, for communication is central to his leadership ability, and this system of government does not function well without strong presidential leadership.

Those sentences sum up what President Reagan was able to do: to articulate a vision for America and to translate this vision into a specific set of goals to lead this country. He kept the promises that he made, not in 1980, but that he had been making basically since 1964. He did what he said he was going to do. We used to remind those people who criticized Reaganomics that this President said he was going to try to cut spending and cut taxes, and he did what he set out to do. He did not promise one thing and then do something else—a trait found in many officeholders. President Reagan developed a set of themes he felt would bring people together, what I would call a community of values.

It is important to keep in mind that this was the first president to serve a full eight-year term since President Eisenhower, and for many people a two-term presidency was a new institution. What does it mean and how does a president have to change some of the objectives from the first four years to the second four years, when he immediately becomes a lame duck the day after he is reelected to serve the final four-year term? That situation was different, and it was something a president had to recognize and deal with in shaping the presidential message.

President Reagan's inauguration speech in 1981 was the beginning point that put into focus what he wanted to do. I was standing there with the temperature in single digits that January morning as he spoke on the west front of the Capitol. At the speech, President Reagan laid out his feeling for America and the things he wanted to accomplish. He talked about Reaganomics and balancing the budget—or trying to balance it—as one of his goals. He also talked about rebuilding military strength and reinvigorating the interest that Americans have in serving in the military and the American role in shaping the world and making democracy once more something of which to be proud and using it as a governing alternative. He also talked about how to get the government off people's backs by removing regulations and allowing people to do things on their own and for government not to hold back but to allow people's creative genius to move forward. That is the essence of his presidential message and goals that he used to guide his administration. Right or wrong, whether one agreed or disagreed with some of the things he did, no one in this country can ever say that Ronald Reagan did not tell them what he was going to try to do.

An interesting article in the *New York Times* covered a speech that President Reagan made at a Georgetown University convocation. The first two or three paragraphs said that Ronald Reagan said some of the same things he had said in 1981. To me, it is refreshing that this man who had been in office for almost eight years still remembers the core things that got him there, the things that he told the country he wanted to do. He still is driven by those same goals. Consistency is important as one talks about leadership and laying out a vision or direction for the country.

Just how does a president communicate? On the Hill, there are 535 individual newsmakers, any one of whom wants to be on the news on a given night or thinks he or she could be the president someday, versus one newsmaker who sits down at the other end of Pennsylvania Avenue, the President of the United States. When a person works at the White House, he or she learns quickly that there is a big difference between one end of Pennsylvania Avenue and the other. When we were on the Hill, we were accustomed to reporters basically listening to phrases, picking up a phrase here and there, and reporting it or using it for guidance or direction. At the White House where the president is the primary newsmaker, however, the media hang on every syllable one says. Sometimes things do not even have to be said; they look into your face, and if you are frowning or they ask a question and you shrug your shoulders, they read that as some type of communication.

When working at the White House one also realizes the impact that one person or those working for him can have, not just in the United States, but around the world. During the first economic summit in April 1987, Senator Baker had been in office as chief of staff for about two-and-a-half months. At that time questions arose about the Iranians using silkworm missiles supplied by China. We were standing outside the Vatican, and a reporter asked Senator Baker what he thought the policy of the United States should be in dealing with silkworm missiles. He replied that the Orkin strategy should be used. I looked at him; I was not sure what he meant, but he was trying to make a joke. He was talking about Orkin, the pest control company. Within minutes, the press put out a wire headline that said, "Chief of Staff Makes Light of Silkworm Missiles." Senator Baker came running up and said, "What did I do wrong? I always talk that way; don't they know I was kidding?" That is an example of the difference between being at the White House and being a member of Congress. The press are waiting for whatever a person who sometimes acts as the president's spokesman says, and if that person makes light of an issue, the press assumes that the president shares that attitude. A person's words and inflections count for a great deal more when working at the White House. We were very careful from that point forward. We still had some fun and enjoyed ourselves, but we recognized that one had to be very careful in their choice of words.

Thus, there is one news source that I think is important, but one other way the White House is different from the Hill is a responsibility the President has to try to make sure his point of view is communicated to the American people. Having dealt with the media and having been on the media's side of the fence, I can say that it is an adversarial relationship. The press's job is to look at a situation, take it apart, and try to interpret it for the American people—not to tell them what to think, but to try to give them at least some of the thoughts that went into the policy or action and then hope they are led to a appropriate decision. For instance, I do not think the press tells the people how to vote, but they try to influence the decisions the people make in reaching the decision of whom they will vote for on election day.

When a person works for the president, he or she should at least give him his time at bat—let him get his words out there. Some people call it spin control, and some call it orchestrating; I call it doing the job you were hired to do because if you do not get the message out, I don't know who would. There is nothing wrong with a presidential initiative being well explained and then allowing the press to take the information and decide how they want to portray it. I do not agree that a presidential staff should stand mute and allow someone else to supplant their initiatives with his or her own. Thus, whether it is spin control or whatever one calls it, I to think it is important to get the presidential point of view out, to have some direction and look at not just the present, but two, three, and sometimes four months in the future to determine how today's events could be used to influence things the president's administration will be doing several months later. At the White House, nothing is totally separate from anything else. They build on each other. If one gets mired in a ditch, spinning the wheels will not get that person out; he or she has to figure out how to get going again, which is what President Reagan's staff had to do in handling the Iran-contra situation.

President Reagan walked into the TV era full bore. In recalling the images and visual pictures people saw as President Reagan campaigned around the country in 1980, it is apparent that television came into its own in that presidential election. Many times the visual image was as strong or stronger than the spoken work. Television was the medium. Other forms of journalism, particularly newspapers, changed and adapted to what television could do, which was to have an immediate impact on disseminating information to the American people. The *Los Angeles Times* survey a couple of years ago said that 65 percent of the people in this country get their national news from television.

For newspapers to continue to compete, and I hope they do, they have to get past the 30-second news bite that appears every evening and read past the headlines and get more understanding about why decisions are made. Newspapers are creating the news analysis piece that used to be on the editorial page but is now found on the front page; it is someone's opinion that does a great deal more in explaining the how and why behind a situation the traditional "who, what, where, when" that goes into a news story. Moving articles from the editorial page to the front page is the one way I found that newspapers tried to compete in a television age. They seem to be saying, "We also want to talk about why certain things happen and how they happen." That is what television does. Television reports include good pictures, but it the last ten seconds with someone like Sam Donaldson standing on the White House lawn telling what really happened that hits where it counts. He is doing a news analysis of what the pictures mean.

The President in working with television was able to craft a message that would work with the television pictures. He was able to recognize that if there were many American flags behind him and he talked about patriotism and what moves this country, the image served to reinforce his message. The setting does matter because people can keep an image in their minds when a visual is added to the spoken word.

Leslie Stahl commented that she had done a story about how President Reagan's words did not fit with what he was doing, that he would stumble every now and then, and that he would misstate himself. After her piece aired on CBS News, she received a call from the White House congratulating her. In her surprise, she asked, "Why are you doing this? I thought it was one of the toughest pieces I've ever done." The response was, "But the pictures were nice. If you tune the sound out and look at the pictures, the pictures tell the story, not the words," and that is true.

Consider the Labor Day kickoff for the 1988 presidential campaign and the visual image that was projected. George Bush, in an open car at Disneyland with American things around him versus Mike Dukakis standing in Detroit, locked arm-in-arm with labor leaders. The visuals said it all, and I think one impact President Reagan has had is, how does one work with TV and how does one use TV to his benefit? Television clearly became one of the primary tools he used to get his message out and therefore manage to lead the country.

President Reagan also looked at some of the other techniques that previous presidents had used, and I think he chose not to use some of them, such as the press conference. For this President, the press conference was not the best means for him to communicate because it became more of an endurance contest than a way to get facts out about a particular decision. It reminded me of "Stump the Star," a program in which each television correspondent wanted to get up and say, "Can I give you the one where you make the gaffe and then your staff is going to have to spend the next day or so undoing it?" rather than trying to sit and figure out what President Reagan had been doing that people really cared about and wanted to know more about. It should be attributed to this administration's downside that they made the press conference a prime-time event by putting it on at 8:00 p.m. so everyone could see it. One has to keep in mind that such a creation can also become one's greatest enemy. In the case of the press conference, I do not think anyone can control what questions Sam Donaldson or Chris Wallace will ask. I also don't think the circumstances or expectations of the press conference can be controlled, and there is a realization that "this is not the best way to get the President's message out."

When I went to the White House with Senator Baker, we talked about trying to make the President more accessible, not just in terms of press conferences, but in trying to find other outlets for him to get his message to the American people. We received much criticism after four or five months because a press conference had not been held since we had arrived. As we were trying to deal with the dilemma of whether to go ahead and hold a press conference or withstand the pressure and say that the time was not right, we chose to withstand the pressure. The lawyers advised us that if the President were asked questions about the Iran-contra affair, all that he would be able to say would essentially be, "My lawyers have told me I can't answer that." If the President of the United States responds to a question 75 percent of the time by saying, "I can't answer that," the American people will think he is hiding something. We managed to restore President Reagan's ability to recapture the agenda, but this feat could not have been done by responding with "no comment" to the questions asked. The press conference that had been crafted into a prime-time event thus to some extent came back to haunt the President because it was obviously not the best way to get the President's message out at that time.

President Reagan used the photo opportunity to substitute for the press conference. I was reminded sometime ago by a researcher in the White House who worked for President Nixon that President Nixon, not President Reagan, created the "photo op." President Reagan perfected the photo op and used it not just in office, but also in campaigns. Lyn Nofziger, the campaign press aide, would often stop the President on a street corner and have him answer questions. It kept him from going through the day-to-day barrage that Mike Dukakis endured and finally decided was not to his benefit of having the press ask questions rather than a candidate or president being able to outline the things he wanted to discuss.

Ronald Reagan was able to use this method in the campaign of 1980 and carry it into office as well. It afforded him some control of the message. The photo op can become an embarrassment at times, however, if a president is sitting in the Oval Office with a foreign leader and the press shouts out questions. The photo op did become the basic tool that President Reagan used to communicate day-to-day. It was an imperfect but more manageable way for the President to get his message out.

Another option available to President Reagan was the Oval Office speech, which was purely unfiltered Reagan. There is no one taking down his words and translating them and no one who is asking him a question. It is the President delivering whatever message he wants to convey. I have never found a better person to look into that camera lens and have it speak his language than Ronald Reagan. I marveled as he did videotapes. He would have a session about every two weeks. He would walk into the room cold, the words would be put on the teleprompter, and if he had to be four minutes and 58 seconds, he would finish in exactly four minutes and 58 seconds. He knew how to read a script and how to time it and pace himself so that he could fit it within a certain time period. He also knew how to make friends with the camera. The Oval Office speech for him was the television format to deliver the message and provide that forum for leadership.

There was a concern about going to the well too often, which is what happened around the time of the Iran-contra episode. While President Reagan was a great communicator, one must be careful in using him as *the communicator*. If a person is too visible, when it is important to make a point, the impact may be missed. If a major issue arises and the president delivers the message at the appropriate time, it will have an impact. An example would be the way President Reagan rallied the country to support his tax cuts in 1981. But if *every* time an issue comes up the president delivers the message, I believe it waters down the appeal over time. A president would not have the same kind of leadership or the same ability to lead because his messages would become matter of fact.

President Reagan used the Oval Office speech and the weekly radio address as his principle means to converse with the American people. When the Iran-contra episode occurred, the President appeared ill-prepared in his public appearances, and suddenly the President was not heard from for four months. That absence went a long way toward creating the impression in the minds of many people in the United States that there must have been more to the problem than they had been told. President Reagan had been there in good and bad times—when the space shuttle went down, when American soldiers died in the Persian Gulf, and to celebrate this country's heritage when he looked at the Statue of Liberty. This President became a symbol for the moods of America, and his voice drove the messages that provided leadership in this country. When suddenly his voice was gone, it had a tremendous impact on the people of this country. The impact was felt from November 1986 until March 1987, when the man who had been there in good times and bad was nowhere to be seen or heard. He was still in the White House, and I believe people hoped he would be able to tell them what really happened and make it right again. Instead, questions kept coming up, and no one was there to answer them. The impact was to leave many people still questioning whether they knew all of the facts and whether the President was telling them everything he knew. When this crisis hit, unlike previous times, the President was not there.

When the President is the one who delivers the message most of the time, he suffers the consequences when he is absent, which is what happened in the Iran-contra affair. People need to realize, however, that a case like Iran-contra teaches them that all choices must be faced—good and bad. If a president is a good communicator and uses his ability to deliver the message, he needs to step up in the tough political battle, as Iran-contra was, and decide how to deal with the problem, how to set it straight, and how to get the country and the presidency going again.

When we went to the White House, many people, particularly in the press, were saying that this presidency might be over, that the country might be waiting for the next presidential election, and that the presidency was going to be on hold for almost two years. Part of what we had to do was to dispel those notions, but also to get Ronald Reagan reestablished as the one setting the tone and the direction and seen as a person who still had much to accomplish, that his best years were not over. That meant putting him before the public where he could use his skill as a communicator to lead the American people as he had done in the past.

Communication—meaning the spoken words—for President Reagan was essential. It was the way he chose to lead this country: through the vision that he laid out, trying to present the choices to the American people and explaining fully what his goals and aspirations were for this country, saying, "This is what America is all about. This is what people in this country care about; this is what people in this country hope to achieve in the future." Not everyone who serves in the Oval Office is going to be like President Reagan and have his ability to lead by communication.

Television has an immediate impact, and to perform the duties and responsibilities of a president, a governor, or a mayor, the relationship must be understood. That medium is part of what one must work with if he or she is to achieve broad public goals. In the 1988 election, there has been extensive reporting about the candidates avoiding issues. I hope that Bush and Dukakis in the next debate will have more time to discuss the issues rather than throwing one-liners at each other. They are using the techniques from the campaign trail, however, expressing their ideas in 20-second sound bites.

Whoever is in the White House next has to also use some of the same criteria as did President Reagan: Is television a friend or enemy? Are you a good manipulator? Do you have a visual image, or is it better for one to find other ways to get a message to the American people? It is important for each president to know their communication strengths and how to incorporate them into their administration. Just as President Reagan was very good on having a set of concise objectives he wanted to accomplish, he was not as detail-oriented as President Carter. But President Reagan could talk about his broad vision for America, whereas President Carter could talk about the individual intricacies of running the government. President Reagan understood his strengths and how to make those strengths available for public consumption.

In a Chattanooga newspaper column today, Tom Wicker picks up a line from Harry Truman: "Truman said that the powers of the presidency amount to trying to persuade the people to do the things they ought to have sense enough to do without my persuading them. That's not a job for a man paddling along in some poll taker's mainstream; that's a job for a leader, someone not afraid to hold up a standard to point the way, even on occasion to swim against the tide." That is what President Reagan did. Whether people agree or disagree with his policies, I do not think one can slight him for having been willing to swim against the tide. He understood what that meant and how, if he were to have an impact and be a leader, if not to control completely, he needed the ability at least to have a hand on the lever that provides direction.

QUESTION: I think most people are fully aware of the significance of rhetoric and communications skills, especially on the part of President Reagan to get his point across. To what extent can rhetoric and communication aides help a president improve rhetoric and communications skills? It seems to me there is an inherent talent involved, that if one is very skilful like President Reagan it could be done. Mr. Carter loved to talk about the many details, and he did that during his administration and last year when he came to the Miller Center. It seems to me that certain communication skills are inherent. How could a president in office be helped to develop those skills?

MR. GRISCOM: If a staff functions properly, it complements the strengths that a president brings to office. I the president were detail-oriented, his staff would have to support the way he wanted to communicate. The worst thing politicians can do is to come in and become something they are not. When that happens, it raises the question of whether that person is hiding something or trying to overlook something that may be very much part of character and very much part of the process that one goes through to make decisions. A staff member should adapt to that person and his style. In the case of President Reagan, his years of training got him to the point where he could stand up and deliver a speech. The written word was only about 10 percent of what he could do once he got in front of a mike to deliver it. He had a very strong delivery.

Some of the things someone in my staff position can do include: go to Moscow and talk to Soviet citizens and talk to U.S. citizens who are stationed in the Soviet Union about their goals and aspirations and what they think of this country and match their responses with President Reagan's actions of the past eight years. We talked tough at times, but that early show of strength has brought us to the point where we could sign the first actual reduction in nuclear arms—not just control them, but reduce them. You pull all of those pieces together and recognize that the President can probably stand in front of a group of students at Moscow State University whom he has never seen and disarm them by being willing to take questions, something that they own leaders have never done in their own country.

The staff attempts to complement the strengths of the president. In the case of Moscow State University, we recognized that the Soviet Union was in a time of change—and in looking at what has happened, it is apparent that it continues to change. Change is very difficult in that country. The people are concerned that by changing, they will lose traditions and things that have been important to them over the years. The American people have a president who can talk about the fact that America is a country of change, that people from around the world come here and relocate in this country with a chance to do things that they wanted to do in their own countries but couldn't for various reasons. Then students in that audience will say they did not realize that America was a country made up of immigrants. There is also a chance for this President, because of his ability to communicate, to talk about the United States and what it is all about and present a little civics lesson inside the speech. We were able to give the students a better feel for what Americans believe and what their hopes are and that we are not sitting over there waiting to push a button to blow them up and that we hope they are not sitting there waiting to push a button to blow us up. We had a chance to explain more about what this country is founded on and to reinforce the point by leaving a copy of the works of Jefferson, Washington, and Lincoln in the Moscow State University Library.

If a staff works properly, it takes the strengths of the president as well as the weaknesses and builds around them. One does not try to re-create something that is not there because it would not come across as genuine; it would come across as very hollow in the process. Because President Reagan had core convictions and some basic principles for which he stood along with an ability to stand up and speak, there was a foundation on which to build, and that is what we were able to do.

QUESTION: To what extent do the postwar American presidents spend time and energy polishing their rhetoric and communication skills?

MR. GRISCOM: I think television changed things in this country because of communication; information could be disseminated immediately. Presidents had to recognize and deal with new journalists who were on-the-spot commentators. In a country where public opinion is very important, if a president is trying to shape policy and does not have public support, it is like swimming upstream and never getting to your destination. In a country where pollsters conduct polls at the drop of a hat, a president must make sure that he has a chance to shape his agenda and get his point of view across. He must ensure that his message is being delivered into homes around the country—and around the world—and that he can help shape and form that message. If one does not use those opportunities, they he has a void; and believe me, the void will be filled.

As communication director for the White House, I had a group that met each morning to review the messages for the day and refine them if necessary. I also had a planning group that drew from all of the major areas within the White House, projecting for as long as four months down the road. We began planning for the Moscow summit the week after the Washington summit ended, thinking then not only about what it was that we might do in Moscow, but also what the events would be leading up to that time. If we were going to talk about individual freedoms in Moscow, shouldn't we at least be setting the scenario and deciding some of the themes in advance? If suddenly we went to Moscow and started talking about something no one had heard before, that would have an impact too. People will often question individual actions a president takes, but they must understand that it is a building process. For instance, if we knew a tough issue such as aid to the contras was coming before Congress, we needed to get President Reagan's message out to help shape the debate, while recognizing that we might not be successful.

QUESTION: I am curious about the cause of the communications breakdown; that is, George Shultz, who was in charge of the State Department, knew what was going on in the Iran-contra affair, yet people inside the White House did not know what was happening.

MR. GRISCOM: I have tried not to criticize those who preceded us in the White House. Don Regan gave us some advice that first Saturday when we went to the White House. He said to get a flak jacket and put it on backwards. I think people expect that a chief of staff knows everything that is going on, and I think he should. People think of a chief of staff as the person who sits beside the president, knows all of the levers being pulled, and can stop them before something happens. That is not the way it works. The chief of staff and the national security adviser have almost equal access to the president. The chief of staff knows what the national security adviser is sending in, but the national security adviser also sends a brown folder in each day that contains the president's security briefing. Sometimes a few other things are included in that folder that the president might want to see, but they are decision memos. Quite often a chief of staff does not even know those other items have been included.

I think the next president needs to sit down and seriously look at the staffing of the White House and the responsibilities that key White House staff should assume. President Reagan gets faulted because he delegated a great deal. I am not sure that this procedure was so wrong. The other side of it is if a president becomes so mired down in details that he loses vision of what he should be doing. A president should have a vision and direction to lead this country; he should have things he really cares about, but that also requires staff that understands their role. It is what I call the Howard Baker rule: No surprises.

In putting the summit together, I met with the President three times so he would know what I was doing and what my ideas were to ensure that he did not get surprised in Moscow. I wanted to make sure he knew what was happening because I think that is the role of a good staff—to make sure your support the president and don't surprise him.

I think several things went awry in the Iran-contra situation. One, I do not think there was ever a clear policy as to what the United States was ultimately trying to achieve in Central America. I will be frank. When the policy was first enunciated, there were those in the administration who felt that our role was to overthrow the Sandinistas. There were those who felt our role was to support the contras and bring pressure to change the government. There were those who felt that we should be out there in some role to prevent the Soviets from establishing a beachhead in Central America. But I don't think any one person ever sat down and made a decision as to what the United States was going to do and then drove the policy to make it happen. Therefore, what occurred was a situation best called a leadership gap. Certain people within the National Security Council (NSC) stepped in and filled that void, and they began trying to drive the policy for what they thought the goal was, which was to ensure that there was a democratic government in Nicaragua. We all know the result.

I would like to know where the communication breakdown occurred. We walked into a White House that was caught up in this situation, and we were trying to sort out very quickly what went wrong. If George Shultz and Cap Weinberger were saying something, why weren't people listening? If the NSC had an operational unit in place, why didn't someone know about it? I have seen the NSC operation, and I know what goes through it; it is hard for me to understand why someone in an oversight role did not catch this, but they didn't. The bottom line is, knowing that it went this way, why didn't someone give the President the information he needed to prevent his publicly adding to the sense of confusion that occurred in November 1986? Those are answers I do not have.

When a new administration comes into office, it should learn from the mistakes of the current administration. One of the real errors I saw was the assumption that a chief of staff is totally responsible for everything that happens to the president without that person having the authority to handle the role. If I had been Don Regan, I would have stood up early and said, "If I'm going to take all the slings and arrows, then I want to have the ability to control them." He did not have that authority. The argument of what the role of the national security adviser is and how does he interact with the chief of staff and the president goes back to the Kissinger days. The national security adviser wants to ensure that he has direct access to the president. I'm not saying he shouldn't have direct access, but I think if the chief of staff bears the responsibility, he should be able to have access to whatever is happening. Otherwise, the same problem arises again and again. The people in the administration should understand the responsibilities they have. To my way of thinking their role is to support the President of the United States to the best of their ability, and if they see something with which they do not agree, they should bring it to the president's attention. That is all one can do. If the president then decides to move forward, as the president and commander in chief, he has that right. He was elected by the people to exercise that authority. If problems are not brought to his attention, then the staff person responsible for that omission has not fulfilled his or her job as a staff person. Regardless of who is in office, there are so many details and so many things happening so fast that no president can know everything to the nth degree all of the time. That is why a president needs good people to support him. I hope that is one of the lessons that comes out of the Reagan administration.

QUESTION: When you were talking about press conferences in the Reagan presidency, it seemed as though you had a one-way notion;

that is, that the function of a press conference is for the president to get his message out. It seems to me that he can get his message out with one of the Oval Office speeches. To me, the whole notion of a press conference is give-and-take. It is a responsibility that the president has to the people as a whole to respond to questions from the press. In your notion, it is as though he can give press conferences at will, and that is why they are so infrequent. If press conferences are seen as a responsibility, then it seems that they should be more frequent. How would you respond to the idea that there is a responsibility involved?

MR. GRISCOM: I agree with your point. One of the first things Dan Rather said about President Reagan when we went to the White House was that the test of whether he could still govern was going to depend on whether he could take questions from the White House press corps. I thought that was going too far. There has to be some common ground between the president and the press, particularly the White House press, so that common terms can be arrived at as to what the press's role is in relaying news and information to the American people. In addition, there must be consideration of the president's responsibility in making sure that he does not get so caught up that he loses his ability to be able to say, "I can't answer that." That type of situation could cause a perception problem for the president and could make people think he was hiding something. I do not advocate doing away with the press conference; I don't think it should be eliminated. I think a press conference is an appropriate training ground and keeps one current, active, and agile with what is occurring and what people are concerned about.

When Senator Baker opened the Senate each day, he had five-to-ten minutes on the floor in front of the chamber with the press about what was happening that day. I think that is something the next president should think about doing. Each morning the president could start the day by bringing 10 or 15 reporters into the Oval Office, alternating among them, and say, "I want to give you something that I'm going to be doing today," and then sit and listen and answer their questions.

I am making two points about press conferences. First, forget the idea that a press conference is a prime-time event. I mentioned that I think this administration made that mistake because a press conference at 2:00 p.m. is just as good as one at 8:00 p.m. The focus should be more on audience share than quality of questions in prime time. The other thing is to take the press conference outside of the White House. What is wrong with coming to Charlottesville and having a press conference or going to Chicago or somewhere else? Who ever said that the only ones to ask the president a question are those people who cover the White House on a day-to-day basis? During the time we were there, two press conferences were held outside the White House, and they were the best press conferences I saw because the questions reflected what was really on the minds of people in this country instead of what a person might say to get on the news that night. I don't think that every press conference should require that the television networks ask questions.

Over the past eight years, 80 percent of the press corps covering President Reagan have never had a chance to ask him a question at a press conference. Why is it that TV correspondents are perceived as having the best questions? I don't think they do, but how can that opinion be changed? How can the press conference be changed from a television spectacle event into an event that provides information to the public and answers their questions? One solution might be for people to call in from time to time and talk to the President. What I want to see is more back and forth conversation that gets questions on the minds of the certain reporters in this country, not necessarily what is on the minds of the ones who cover the White House day-to-day and what may get them on the news that night.

QUESTION: When President Ford followed Nixon, there was a sense of decency and a fresh air blowing through the White House. There was a feeling that when Senator Baker followed Donald Regan of a sense of greater credibility, an impression of clean air coming through. It didn't seem to happen. Were Senator Baker's hands tied too tightly?

MR. GRISCOM: I think the conventional wisdom in Washington was that the bad guys were being replaced by "one of our own" because Senator Baker had been serving for 18 years and everything would suddenly change. What people seemed to forget was that we were brought in to deal with the tough political problem for

President Reagan of trying to get his agenda back on track. Accomplishing that task would mean some tough decisions would have to be made and that the administration was not going to be able to say, "We are just going to forget about this," or "Whatever you ask for we are going to give you."

The veto of the Highway Bill, which occurred during the first two weeks we were there, was heavily criticized. Many people asked why Senator Baker let that happen, saying that it was a no-win situation. People lost sight of the fact that there was still a president in the Oval Office who was actually going to be president. Our job was to give him the best advice we could and work with him. That approach was Senator Baker's strength, that he was not going to try to replace the President with his own thinking, but to try to give the President his best advice, and once a decision was made, to carry it out. While the administration might have acted differently on the Highway Bill, the President made a choice; he fought a good fight and lost by one vote. It showed that he was still ready to fight. He went to the Senate, spoke to the Republican senators trying to get that last vote, and after it was over, even Senator Kennedy commended the President for his conviction in standing by what he believed.

In some quarters of Washington, people forgot that everything was not removed when we became part of the staff. The only thing changed was that Don Regan left with some of his key staff. Senator Baker and two or three others replaced them. The playing field was exactly the same; we were trying to level it again, but in doing so we had to deal with the existing circumstances. I guarantee that if we could have started over, we would have gotten a big eraser and said, "Iran-contra is gone; let's get rid of it." Some of the toughest work I have ever done is having to sit there day in and day out and figure out what to do to make sure that (1) the story is kept out of the White House as much as possible; (2) the President's interests and point of view is protected and gotten across; and (3) although he had many things to accomplish, he could still drive an agenda and be a part of the Washington structure that would make things happen and set policy in this country. That is the situation when we arrived.

Part of our mistake—if I can term it that—was in allowing the perception that suddenly things would be different with Senator Baker and others of us becoming part of the administration. We later decided that more should have been done to hold down that expectation level because we knew beforehand what problems we would have to handle and that in doing so we would not be the ultimate decisionmakers. The President of the United States was, and we had to follow his direction after we gave him our advice. It is very different when someone at the top makes the final choice instead of being a U.S. senator and making decisions yourself.

QUESTION: Many people were surprised when Senator Baker dropped out of the presidential primary race and took the job as chief of staff. Could you explain why he made that decision?

MR. GRISCOM: I think Senator Baker feels strongly that when a president asks a person to do something, that person is obligated to do it. When President Reagan asked Senator Baker to become chief of staff, he felt he could not say no. He feels that any American should feel a sense of duty and responsibility when the President of the United States asks them to make a sacrifice. In this case it was for him to give up his opportunity to enter the presidential race. In the final analysis, he said, "How would I set aside what the President asked me to do to help him in return for something that I might want to do but might not be successful in achieving?" He thus decided that the answer was, if the President asks, one must say yes. I think he President Reagan asked him again today to come back, he would drop what he was doing and go back one more time.

QUESTION: The scholars of the presidency have called attention to the emergence of the form of communication where presidents no longer address policies to Congress, but will often go over the heads of Congress and appeal directly to the people and have them bring pressure to bear on the legislature. You alluded to the contra-aid fight. Part of the downside that scholars have pointed out is that regardless of what amount of capital a president may have, how many congressmen would back that? I wonder if contra aid would be a good example of this type of situation and whether to the extent you were involved in mapping out the speeches in which the President did appeal directly to the public in that fashion, were you concerned about conserving some of that capital for future use, and what kinds of attempts were made to ensure that he would not exhaust his reserves?

MR. GRISCOM: I made the point that the President's message became very diluted because the administration kept using him as the only means to communicate. Why not let the attorney general, secretary of state, or secretary of the treasury bear some of the burden of getting the message out and then bring the president in when he is really needed to have an impact?

In the case of Iran-contra, we were going against public opinion because the policy was never fully worked out. At that point the White House staff said that there was no one else with any credibility left who could talk about it other than the President, so they felt he would have to do so. We questioned whether or not to go forward with that appeal. The networks all refused to carry it. They said it wasn't newsworthy, and that also troubled me. I asked at what point television people became not only reporters of a story but also judges of its newsworthiness. They answered that if the President would add this to his speech, they would cover it. I thought that was stepping way over the boundary that exists between the media and an officeholder, who in this case happened to be the President. There were certain people who were trained to say that the only one who could deliver the message was the President. Many of them were conservative followers of President Reagan who essentially said, "If you don't use him then you are not using all of the abilities that you have to try to move public opinion, and therefore we are going to be critical of you and are going to let it be known that the White House held back from using the President." Thus, we had to deal with these kinds of pressures as well.

We ran into that often with the nominations to the Supreme Court of Bork, Ginsburg, and Kennedy. I know this situation quite well because I sat in the Roosevelt Room and had to tell Judge Bork that the President was not going to do a televised speech immediately before the committee vote on his nomination. There was no doubt as to what was going to happen—that they were going to give him an unfavorable vote. If one delivers the best shot then, it cannot be retracted when the vote gets to the full Senate. The President used all of the influence and persuasion he had, and the committee still voted him down. Many people have a hard time understanding that one must hold back for impact at times, and if the President himself is the object of greatest impact, he cannot be throw in the spotlight helter-skelter.

Maybe a president should decide in the beginning of his first term whether he plans on being a four-year or an eight-year president and then map out a strategy for moving his agenda. At what point should someone else carry a message for the president so that when the television networks decide to air it, they won't say that they had heard him talk about it time and time again. That is the dilemma the administration ran into with the Contra-aid battle in the final analysis.

QUESTION: I understand that you wrote the speech at Moscow State University that was originally to be broadcast across the Soviet Union but was not. Was the speech previewed by the officials in the Soviet Union? What difference would that have made in the preparation of the speech if it had been known that the audience would be college students versus the whole nation?

MR. GRISCOM: The speech was not reviewed in advance. We had hoped that they would broadcast it, but they made the comment that they had technical problems and thus could not broadcast it. I'll let you decide for yourselves what that explanation was worth. We were disappointed because we wanted President Reagan to have a chance to talk to the whole Soviet Union. Whether they rebroadcast it or not, as they told us they were going to do, I have yet to find out.

I guess in the final analysis that after having allowed 600, 700, or 800 college students in the Soviet Union hear the President, there is no way they could say don't believe him after the speech. I had said it would have been much better to broadcast the speech over the entire country, but the college-student audience was the best setting because they were young people and were thus the future leaders of the country. They would be raising questions with the current leaders about why they had been taught one thing and the President of the United States was allowed to come in and tell them something different. They will have to wrestle with that question and reconcile the differences that exist.

I know the speech was reprinted and passed out in other cities in the Soviet Union by some U.S. embassy people, but clearly the ability to have had it broadcast would have been preferable. If President Reagan gets rebroadcast, the same thing that occurred with Tom Brokaw's interview with Gorbachev could happen again: Gorbachev's answers were edited. People hearing a rebroadcast of what President Reagan said may not get the total context in which he said it.

We learned that we should push harder the next time around. When we initially raised the idea of doing the Moscow State University speech, after we said the President would make some prepared remarks and then have a Q&A, there was silence. The person with whom I was negotiating asked, "What is a Q&A?" I answered that it was the time in which the President would take questions from the audience and respond to them. They huddled for a minute and came back and said, "Who is going to write the questions? Is he going to write them himself and answer them?" We answered no, that they would do it. They held another small conference, came back, and said, "We write the questions and give them to him?" I said for them to do whatever they wanted to do and that all we were asking was that after he makes the speech, the President be allowed to have students—not 40-, 50-, or 60-year-old men—stand up and ask questions from the audience for him to answer. The idea that we meant for the President to answer the questions right after his prepared remarks was very foreign to them. They had never seen this happen. I found it interesting that after the President's session with the students, during the same summit week General Secretary Gorbachev held the first press conference in the Soviet Union that had ever been conducted by a general secretary.

It is small things such as this occasion that may be opening up the Soviet Union for a freer exchange of ideas. If it only an incremental movement, at least there is some impact.

QUESTION: It seems that Reagan's policies are increasingly generating a political process by trying to turn political events into entertainment and by broadcasting press conferences during prime time. The emphasis is image rather than substance. Is there any solution to this problem, or is it just going to get worse and worse?

MR. GRISCOM: Unfortunately, people in office and those campaigning for office have to fit into that environment because most news is delivered to the American people in 20- or 30-second sound bites. A couple of things need to be changed. First, people, particularly young people, need to read past the headlines and find out what is happening rather than simply glancing at television news. A couple of weeks ago, we were discussing at the University of Tennessee a certain event that had been discussed on "Night Line," and the students repeated almost verbatim what had been said on "Night Line." I said, "Fine; now tell me what it meant," and there was no response. What troubles me is that we are not stimulating people enough to think past the headlines or the sound bite to want to ask questions and find out more on their own. People need to reeducate themselves so that they can read past what they are being told for greater understanding.

Also, I hope there will be more presidential debates, but they should have a different structure. Instead of relying exclusively on journalists as questioners, the two candidates should quiz each other. It may be knock-down-and-drag-out, but what is wrong with that? What is wrong with them sitting and probing each other and asking other questions, such as, "Why did you say this?" Maybe people would hear more than Joe Isuzu answers and a Boston Harbor one-liner. Why didn't someone the other night talk about what the United States is going to do about its trade situation? Why don't the candidates press each other and say, "What are you going to do about the deficit in this country? How are you going to deal with it? Are you going to put Social Security off-limits?" Those questions have to be wrestled with, but we are not getting those answers. Part of it is because "we the people" get the type of government and the type of coverage we deserve.

If the American people would become outraged at the media, as they did when the media went after Quayle, and tell them they went too far, the media would begin retreating. People should say, "We want to know more and hear more. We want to see more than just a nice visual image. We want to know what is going on." Why not call on television particularly to provide an opportunity in that forum for more of a public affairs approach than just an attempt to capsule things? People need to demand more news coverage than they are now receiving. Otherwise, they will end up with the same type of campaign that is going on right now, which is the candidates trying to decide where they can get the best picture so that when people see it broadcast, they will be looking at *where* someone was, not necessarily *what* it was that they said.

NARRATOR: We thank you for a most challenging presentation.

CHAPTER 5

THE REAGAN ADMINISTRATION: WHITE HOUSE CONTROL OF DOMESTIC POLICY*

SHIRLEY ANNE WARSHAW

NARRATOR: We have talked quite a bit about governance at the Miller Center in recent months, and yet we have not had many speakers who deal with the interaction of units within the single branches of government. It is partly for that reason we are pleased to have Professor Shirley Anne Warshaw speak to us about White House control of domestic policy.

Dr. Warshaw is a professor of political science at Gettysburg College, where she was director of the Dwight D. Eisenhower Symposium. She is now director of the Washington Programs and associate director of the Eisenhower Leadership Center at Gettysburg College. Dr. Warshaw holds a doctorate from Johns Hopkins University, a master's degree from the Wharton School of Finance and Commerce, and a bachelor's degree from the University of Pennsylvania.

Her publications include *The Eisenhower Legacy, Re-examining the Eisenhower Presidency*, and a forthcoming book, *Power Sharing: Cabinet Government in the Modern Presidency*. She has also been a contributor to the volumes published by the Hofstra University conferences on the presidency.

Presented in a Forum at the Miller Center of Public Affairs on 2 November 1993.

Dr. Warshaw served as a consultant to the Domestic Policy Council of the White House and the National Advisory Council for the Center for the Study of the Presidency in New York, of which she is a member. She was a consultant to PBS for the six-hour series on the Eisenhower legacy. She is also a member of the Finnegan Foundation Board of Directors and serves on the Program Committee for the Eisenhower World Affairs Institute. Thus, she brings a rich background to our subject.

When I mentioned to Herbert Brownell that Dr. Warshaw had accepted our invitation he said, "That is wonderful. She is very able." Praise from Herbert Brownell is something all of us respect.

MS. WARSHAW: Thank you for that wonderful introduction. I am focusing most of my work right now on White House-Cabinet relations in the modern presidency, which begins with Nixon. I have interviewed most of the White House staff and Cabinet in almost every administration since Nixon. My topic is the Reagan administration. All of the Reagan Cabinet members have received copies of each piece I have written on Reagan. My focus in particular has been how the White House controls policy-making in the domestic arena, not in the foreign policy arena. I shall present an overview of the recent White House-Cabinet structures established for domestic policy-making.

Remembering all of the campaigns in recent years, every president has argued that the power of the White House staff should be reduced, with more policy-making power given to the Cabinet. This trend began in the Johnson years. There was no White House staff before Franklin Delano Roosevelt created one with the Reorganization Act. Roosevelt, Truman, and Eisenhower, however, did not build a significant White House staff. Of those three presidents, Eisenhower was the first to take serious action in that direction. For instance, he created the positions of press secretary, scheduler, and Cabinet secretary—not numerous positions, but quite a few nonetheless. Under John F. Kennedy the White House staff grew somewhat, but most of the true expansion occurred in the Johnson years. It was Joe Califano who first began to gain control of policy-making at the White House level.

The White House began to gain control of policy-making in direct relationship to the increase in the federal budget. The federal budget was $9 billion in 1940. At that time, there was not much of a role for the federal government. We saw states' rights and states' activism controlling the policy process. Then with the New Deal, the federal government emerged as a policymaker. That role grew continuously, only suffering a short hiatus during the Eisenhower administration when the Republican minority in Congress, led by Congressman Halleck, urged the federal government not to take a dominant role in policy-making, but instead leave it to the states. The federal government nonetheless again became the focus of policy-making during the Kennedy era. Kennedy began to build a White House staff, and that staff proliferated in the Johnson years.

Richard Nixon, however, campaigned on a pledge to build a Cabinet government. He saw the Great Society as totally White House-based and wanted to reverse that trend. He wanted to reverse the movement of policy-making into the White House and give it back to the departments and back to the states with a new federalism. His pledge was to rebuild a strengthened Cabinet, put policy-making back in the Cabinet, and reduce the role of the White House staff. In part, he hoped this change would begin a trend back to a state-oriented policy-making system.

Nixon, therefore, began his administration with a Cabinet-based system. He brought in Daniel Patrick Moynihan as his assistant for urban affairs. Moynihan also did limited policy-making in the White House. Part of this change was because Richard Nixon firmly believed the president's time needed to be spent on foreign policy. He wanted to reduce the role of the federal government in domestic policy-making, and certainly wanted to reduce the role of the White House staff in domestic policy-making. Richard Nixon soon found, however, that the Cabinet officers were quite easily co-opted by their departments, with the departments pursuing policies that lacked either his political interest or his programmatic interest. By programmatic interest, I mean they were pursuing policies that went against his goal of reducing the role of the federal government in domestic policy-making and certainly against his goal of reducing the federal budget.

For example, Secretary George Romney at HUD actually wanted to see an increased role for what is called the Model Cities Program, which Lyndon Johnson had supported. Richard Nixon went on record during the campaign as opposing Model Cities. George Romney went to Congress and urged the opposite. Furthermore, Robert Finch, the secretary of health, education, and welfare (HEW) and someone in whom Richard Nixon had great personal confidence, supported continuation of social services programs. This was in spite of Richard Nixon's pledge to reduce the role of the federal government in such social services.

There also is the classic case of Walter Hickel. While secretary of the interior he campaigned against the Vietnam War. Without talking to President Nixon, he publicly supported a reduced role for the United States in Vietnam. Hickel also opposed Nixon's idea to locate a major airport just outside the Everglades to service that portion of Florida.

Everywhere he turned, Richard Nixon saw his Cabinet officers being co-opted by their departments. He responded by reducing the policy-making role of the departments and increasing the role the White House staff in policy-making.

Nixon created the Domestic Council through his 1970 executive order. This created an in-house policy mechanism to provide domestic policy advice to the president on a level parallel to the National Security Council, which had been institutionalized and part of the White House staff since 1947. When Nixon created the Domestic Council, he fired Moynihan and Arthur Burns. John Ehrlichman, who became Richard Nixon's chief domestic policy adviser, centralized policy-making in the White House. For the remainder of the Nixon administration we saw a tightly controlled policy process where policy initiatives came out of the White House. Most initiatives by the departments had to be cleared through the White House. As a result, the White House staff burgeoned in size.

The Watergate crisis brought an abrupt end to the Nixon presidency, bringing Gerald Ford into office in August 1974. Ford looked at the huge White House staff that had controlled policy-making and decided it had insulated Nixon and was part of the problem that led to Watergate. Reminiscent of Nixon's 1968 campaign, Gerald Ford promised a decentralized White House staff with a greater reliance on his Cabinet. Ford had a problem, however. He came into office in 1974 with a reinvigorated Cabinet, because the Watergate crisis left the White House staff in such disarray that the Cabinet had become an independent force in policy-making. Ford needed to provide the Cabinet leadership in policy objectives.

Ford moved first to control his own staff. Within a month Haig was reassigned and Donald Rumsfeld was brought in to head the White House staff. When Rumsfeld went to the Defense Department, Ford then made Dick Cheney chief of staff. Each of these people knew they needed to gain control of the policy-making process because the departments were acting in their own interests. For example, the Federal Energy Council, which was a precursor to the Energy Department, was advocating major tax increases for gas, while Gerald Ford was refuting such a tax increase. Gerald Ford was never successful in gaining control of the policy process, primarily due to a difficult White House staff that was full of infighting.

Jimmy Carter entered office also saying that he needed to gain control of the domestic policy process. Carter, however, who viewed Watergate as an example of the problems associated with insulating the president, did as Richard Nixon had done: He gave power to the Cabinet officers. By summer 1979, he also realized that his department heads had been totally co-opted by the Cabinet officers—policies coming out of the departments failed to meet his needs. As in the Nixon administration, there were classic examples of this co-optation. President Carter and Griffin Bell, his attorney general, had essentially the following conversation: President Carter said, "Griffin, you realize that we have an election coming up in 1980, and we have some problems. One of those is a religion problem. I fear we have lost the Catholic vote." Griffin Bell said, "I don't disagree with you. What can we do for you?" Jimmy Carter replied, "I think we can regain the Catholic vote if we can enhance the parochial school system. One way to enhance the parochial school system is to actually provide them some funds." Jimmy Carter's White House staff, through Stu Eizenstat, had developed the idea that they would give the parochial schools CETA funds—funds from the now defunct Comprehensive Employment Training Act. The attorney general, however, argued that giving federal funds to a church-related endeavor violated the First Amendment. Griffin Bell firmly opposed the plan on constitutional grounds.

In the end the parochial schools were given CETA funds, but Carter was furious that the Constitution had been brought into political considerations. One does not think of Jimmy Carter as political, but he was extremely political.

Within about a year and a half, Carter had become so upset with his Cabinet that he fired half of them. He told the Cabinet members who were left that he did not want anything coming out of the departments that wasn't cleared first with Stu Eizenstat. Carter also brought in Hamilton Jordan as his chief of staff, although he had sworn in the campaign that he would never have a chief of staff. So, Hamilton Jordan, Jack Watson, and Stu Eizenstat tightly controlled the development of domestic policy-making.

Ronald Reagan is, in my estimation, the only president in recent years who has really looked at the institution of the presidency and examined the problems the institution has had in policy-making and in its relations with Congress. Reagan essentially promised to build a relationship with the Cabinet. No one since Franklin Delano Roosevelt had built a team approach between a strong White House staff and a Cabinet, as Reagan tried to do. I will be focusing for the remainder of my presentation on what Reagan did to facilitate this strong working relationship between a White House staff and a Cabinet.

If I asked which of all of the recent presidents beginning with Nixon had the strongest presidency, who would you name? Whether you agree or disagree with the programs that came out of each presidency, which president was most successful in accomplishing what he said he would do? The answer is Ronald Reagan, without question. One of the reasons is because Ronald Reagan knew how to forge strong working relationships among all of the people around him. The great failure of the Ford administration was the terrible jockeying for power among the White House staff. Under Reagan there was no jockeying for power either among the White House staff or between the White House staff and the Cabinet. They all had a single goal in mind. To achieve this unity between the Cabinet and the White House staff, Reagan surrounded himself with people he trusted.

Most of the Cabinet members in the Nixon, Ford, and Carter administrations were not close friends of their respective presidents. Those presidents, particularly Jimmy Carter, wanted to create a political base within the Cabinet. This strategy goes back to the Jacksonian era, which was almost a spoils system. Carter wanted to make sure his Cabinet had women and minorities in it and reflected geographic and ethnic diversities—in short, that the Cabinet represented all of America. To achieve that representation, he brought in people he did not know. He had never met most of those people before their initial meetings.

On the other hand, Ronald Reagan said, "I won, folks, by over 9 percent." Remember that Richard Nixon won by less than 1 percent in 1968, and Gerald Ford was not elected. The Ford-Carter election was a 2.1 percent margin. These people had relatively narrow margins. Ronald Reagan won by 9.7 percent. That is a substantial winning margin, as we all know by watching recent presidents. Reagan said, "I don't need to build any further political bases. I don't need to use my Cabinet to ensure a greater mandate than I already have. I am going to surround myself with people I know, people I trust, people who have the same agenda as I do."

He first brought in an old friend, Pendleton James, who was a Los Angeles personnel recruiter from the same social circles as Reagan. James had been involved with personnel recruitment during the Nixon administration. He had been Frederic Malek's (Richard Nixon's personnel chief) deputy director and thus had internal White House experience. He had external experience as well and was a personal friend of Reagan. Reagan told Pendleton James before the nomination to think about compiling a list of names for key positions in a Reagan administration.

Immediately after Reagan was nominated for the presidency, he provided $80,000 and an office for James in Alexandria, Virginia, with instructions to begin the recruitment process. James began assembling names and met frequently with a group of Reagan's personal friends: Joseph Coors, William French Smith, Caspar Weinberger, and Charles Swift. These people, along with Pendleton James, compiled a list of names for the Cabinet, so they were ready to fill Cabinet posts when Reagan won the election.

None of the people on the list were contacted before the election. They began contacting these people, however, on the day of the election. James had a short list with three questions used to screen prospective Cabinet members: Is he a Reagan man? In other words, had he actively supported the Reagan presidency? Is he a conservative? Not just did he support the Republican ticket, but is he a conservative? Does he support the Reagan agenda? Supporting the Reagan agenda and being conservative were slightly different.

The masculine gender in the above questions was used deliberately because Reagan did not consider women for these posts. We had had a history in recent administrations of including gender diversity in the Cabinet, but women were never seriously considered for the Reagan Cabinet. They appointed Jeane Kirkpatrick as ambassador to the United Nations with Cabinet status, but that is arguable because the ambassador to the United Nations reports to the secretary of state, who has Cabinet status. There would certainly not be two Cabinet people reporting officially one to another. They gave her that status in large part because she was a woman, and they wanted to have a "woman" in the Cabinet.

James chose nearly all of Reagan's Cabinet officers, each of whom had the same focus as Reagan, although Reagan did not necessarily know them personally. They also were all basically the same age as Reagan. He liked to surround himself with people who had a great deal in common with him, which James knew.

There were three exceptions to the Cabinet selection process. One was the secretary of the interior. Senator Paul Laxalt of Nevada, an old friend of Reagan, had asked to choose the person for that position. Laxalt had a sheep farm in Nevada and wanted to ensure that the secretary of the interior was someone he could trust to protect it. James Watt, a farmer in Wyoming, was an old friend of Senator Laxalt, and it was he who received the nomination.

The second exception was the secretary of energy. After Pendleton James had assembled and announced the candidates for Cabinet positions, Strom Thurmond became incensed and said to President Reagan that no one from the South was on the list. Reagan replied that he had not noticed that exclusion. Since the original nominee for secretary of energy had withdrawn, not wanting to have his finances revealed before the Senate, Strom Thurmond asked if he could propose a candidate for that position. Reagan said yes, and Thurmond nominated his friend James Edwards, who was a dentist and former governor of South Carolina.

The third position, the secretary of agriculture, was filled by John Block, with the aid of his friend Bob Dole. A fourth Cabinet candidate, Malcolm Baldrige at the Department of Commerce, was questionable. He was a friend of George Bush, and there was substantial evidence that George Bush supported him. As for the White House staff, Reagan simply moved his three key campaign aides–Ed Meese, Jim Baker, and Michael Deaver–into the White House, as all presidents do.

Thus, the people surrounding President Reagan, both in the White House and the Cabinet, were people of his age and social background with whom he had a great deal in common on a personal level. There was great camaraderie among this group that you did not see in any of the other administrations. Most important, they all shared an absolutely clear view of where they wanted to take the government.

The next step in building this strong White House–Cabinet relationship was to establish an organizational structure which would ensure that the administration had control over the domestic policy process. Reagan needed to ensure that the Cabinet officers did not become co-opted by their departments and did not move in directions other than those the President himself wanted. The first action he took was to increase the size of the White House staff. Previous presidents had taken office and reduced the White House staff. When Reagan assumed office in 1981, there were 51 people on the senior White House staff, which does not include the military staff, the vice president's staff, the first lady's staff, or most of the administrative offices. The White House staff was made up of senior people with titles such as assistant to the president, special assistant to the president, and deputy assistant to the president, who had policy-making responsibilities. In less than a year, that number increased to 82--an increase of more than 50 percent.

Reagan next established what is called the Cabinet Council system, which he did cleverly through an office on the White House staff called the Office of Policy Development (OPD). Nixon had created the Domestic Council to monitor domestic policy-making. Ford had kept the Domestic Council to monitor policy-making. Carter had changed the name to the Domestic Policy Group, but its role remained the same as that of its predecessors, the Domestic Council and the Domestic Policy Group.

More than any other president, however, Reagan really took control of this process. He put Dr. Martin Anderson, an economics professor at Stanford University, in charge of domestic policy-making. Anderson, an assistant to John Ehrlichman and also Arthur Burns in the Nixon administration, had been Reagan's campaign director of economic policy-making. Anderson came into the White House with the objective of developing a careful working relationship between the White House and the Cabinet to ensure absolute control of policy development by the White House. He achieved this objective by creating Cabinet Councils—working groups of Cabinet officers who met weekly to discuss President Reagan's policy options.

The Cabinet Council idea was the key to the centralized policy development system that the Reagan administration set in place. Reagan would focus his Cabinet officers on issues that he wanted to tackle. They would talk about their initiatives and he would voice his approval or disapproval. From the outset of the administration, the Cabinet officers obtained their information from the President. We in political science refer to this strategy as "keeping the Cabinet officers in the presidential orbit." That strategy is very significant; it ensures that the policy remains in the presidential orbit and is not moved out to the departments.

No other president has done this, including George Bush and Bill Clinton. Reagan is the only president in what we call the postmodern presidency who actually sat weekly with his Cabinet officers. We are not talking about Cabinet meetings; he had those too. We are talking about a meeting with each of the different Cabinet councils (a total of five), each council being made up of five or six Cabinet officers. He talked nearly every week with the different members about what he wanted them do to.

Anderson made sure they met regularly. They met in the White House, and the Cabinet officers knew they were part of Reagan's team. The problem with Cabinet officers is they can easily feel they are not part of the president's team but part of the department's team and become department spokesmen to the president. Reagan wanted to ensure that these people were his spokesmen to the department, and subsequently kept in constant contact with them. In understanding the importance of this approach, you should remember that when you are in the department as a Cabinet secretary, you have a magnificent office, many secretaries, a telephone with numerous buttons, and people fawning over you. This attention builds your ego, and suddenly you feel very departmentally based. Then you go to the White House, and you are not a big shot any more; you are just one of a very large group. The White House staffers think they are more important than you are. Thus, an important part of the Reagan administration's effort to control policy-making was reducing the image of the White

House staff and keeping the Cabinet officers aware of their importance in the White House. This balance was very important.

In addition, Anderson established departmental working groups of deputy secretaries. These people did not meet in the departments, but in the Old Executive Building. They also met regularly with Anderson's staff to learn what the Cabinet councils were doing and in which direction Reagan wanted the departments to go. Anderson was trying to gain control not only of the senior level, but also the next level—the undersecretaries, deputy secretaries, assistant secretaries, and so on—to ensure that they too remained presidentially based and not departmentally based.

This massive effort to keep all of these people in the presidential orbit was quite difficult—remember there are 5,000 presidential appointments and 3.5 million people in the federal government, so there are few people that you can really control. Other presidents lost control, even of their 5,000 appointments. Reagan worked hard at maintaining control of all of these people.

Other administrations had abdicated the role of personnel director, allowing the Cabinet officers to bring in their own people. The Reagan White House, however, said it was controlling every one of those 5,000 presidentially appointed jobs, and Pendleton James was going to recruit and approve them all. Every political job in the departments was approved by the White House. The people recruited were, of course, Reagan supporters, absolute conservatives, and supported a narrow political agenda. Whose agenda did those selections mirror? President Reagan's.

Thus, the Cabinet officers and everyone under them were in a very narrow field. All were constantly interacting with White House personnel. This close connection is what the President wanted. In addition, Reagan tried to personally meet the sub-Cabinet officials. He regularly had the sub-Cabinet staff to the White House for White House dinners and White House receptions, and offered them his box at the Kennedy Center or the Ford Theater. Thus, personal loyalty to President Reagan developed among both Cabinet and sub-Cabinet officials.

Reagan also met with that third tier of political executives— really the lowest level of people—every January in Constitutional Hall for two-and-a-half hours. It was called the Executive Forum, and Reagan would talk to them one-on-one. This effort by Reagan inspired enormous loyalty in these officials, the like of which we had not seen before.

Besides having the policy-making process controlled by the White House staff and all key departmental staff controlled from the White House, Reagan also formed the Legislative Strategy Group to assist in moving policy proposals through Congress. Jim Baker and Max Friedersdorf, the congressional liaison, were selected to accomplish this task. If members of Congress did not support a particular policy initiative, rather than submitting that initiative back to the Cabinet, the departments, or the Cabinet councils, Baker and Friedersdorf simply rewrote it on the spot to meet congressional objectives. The Legislative Strategy Group allowed White House proposals to move quickly through the legislative process without going back through the departmental process.

One of the great stumbling blocks in the Clinton administration today is the slow movement in the legislative process. That is because Clinton has reverted back to the Carter system of giving legislative authority to the Cabinet officers. The exception is the health care issue, which the White House is managing. Most other programs are moving through the departments and are having problems both in receiving presidential approval and in being round-tabled to resolve interjurisdictional problems. Baker was very successful at preventing these types of delays, and his cordial working relationship with Max Friedersdorf was extremely helpful.

I cannot emphasize enough the value of chemistry in these working relationships. That chemistry is one thing Pendleton James understood; that is, if you are going to forge a strong group to move an entire nation forward, there has to be one shared vision. These people have to understand where the administration is going, and there must be personal chemistry among them. It is the president's and the White House staff's responsibility to forge that working relationship. If you want to resolve interjurisdictional disputes or complexities in multidepartmental policy initiatives, you need to know the people and have a comfortable working relationship with them. The problem with most administrations is that some department heads do not know each other (note a book written by Hugh Heclo entitled *Government of Strangers*). There are certainly deputy secretaries who do not know each other. A government cannot work effectively if the staff is not acquainted. The personal camaraderie and chemistry that was built in the policy-making centers of Reagan's administration was one of the great successes of his administration.

During the second Reagan administration there was somewhat of a change in that White House policy-making structure. Donald Regan, secretary of the treasury during the first term, became chief of staff. Regan wanted to centralize control of policy-making in his office. That, to some extent, hurt the Reagan administration. Cabinet Councils played less of a role in policy-making and the carefully sculpted White House–Cabinet relationship deteriorated. As a result, the collegiality in policy-making suffered. The White House began to lose control. Howard Baker and Ken Duberstein eventually took over for Donald Regan, and the system quickly reverted back to its original standard. The same strong policy-making system from the first term was back in place for the next two-and-a-half years.

One of the problems of the Bush administration was that George Bush did not attempt to replicate the strong policy development system that had worked so well in the Reagan adminis-tration. Part of the reason was personal, because the Reagan and the Bush staffs disliked each other. It was not so much that they were philosophically opposed, although the Reagan supporters were more conservative than the Bush supporters. President Bush was more liberal on domestic policy and was moved into the conser-vative wing more by politics than by his own personal beliefs. The staff who surrounded George Bush were similarly more liberal and moderate than the Reagan staff. They disliked each other so intensely that any system Ronald Reagan had set in place was thrown out and a different system put in place.

Roger Porter, who was on Reagan's domestic policy staff and later was head of Bush's domestic policy staff, was absolutely cut off from the inner circle. The reasons why Roger Porter was kept out of the loop are a mystery both to me and to those from the Bush administration with whom I have spoken. The general feeling of those I spoke with was that Porter was kept out of the loop primarily because of his ties to Ronald Reagan.

In general, however, the Bush White House did not control the domestic policy process. The departments had substantial control over policy initiatives. As long as those initiatives met the fiscal constraints of Richard Darman and OMB, they moved forward. The White House provided minimal programmatic guidance.

The Clinton administration is continuing the Bush system. On 1 October 1993, President Clinton announced that he was cutting the White House staff by 25 percent and moving to a Cabinet-based policy development system. The role of the White House staff was to "support the Cabinet in their decision making." The policies that emerge from this administration will be Cabinet based.

Bill Clinton may have a great deal of trouble in the next election because he will not be able to forge the kinds of policies he wants. Those policies are departmentally based and may not meet the goals and objectives of his White House, and there will certainly be political conflicts in those goals and objectives. Unless Bill Clinton moves to gain control of the policy process through the White House, he will suffer the same defeat as George Bush.

QUESTION: Could you explain Sam Pierce's role in the Reagan administration?

MS. WARSHAW: I have met with Sam Pierce. He was brought in by Pendleton James with a mandate to cut the funding programs of the Department of Housing and Urban Development, which he did in the beginning of the administration. Eventually, however, Pierce said to Martin Anderson, "I think perhaps there are some programs, specifically Section Eight of the Subsidized Housing Program, that we perhaps should not cut so deeply." Anderson actually supported that position, and the funding for Section Eight of the Subsidized Housing Program increased.

I have often talked to Secretary Pierce about this situation. I asked, "Mr. Secretary, what would you do if Martin Anderson hadn't approved it?" He said, "I'd go to the President." He went to President Reagan on a number of issues, and Pierce said that Reagan supported him most of the time. I said, "What would you have done if the President hadn't supported you?" He said, "That would have been the end of it. I would have done what the President told me to do."

This was true of every one of Reagan's Cabinet officers. If they went to Reagan and he said he did not support their position, they would follow what he wanted to do. In other administrations, the Cabinet officers would not have taken quite so kindly to the President turning off one of their programs, and they would have then gone to their own constituency, whether it be the natural constituents of the department or their natural constituents in Congress.

QUESTION: I thought Reagan once addressed Pierce as "Mr. Mayor." Did he get a little confused?

MS. WARSHAW: The first few Cabinet meetings he would walk by him and not know who he was, so that is very true.

QUESTION: Since you are talking about the presidential staff under various presidents, what numbers in terms of size are we talking about under the presidents whom you have mentioned?

MS. WARSHAW: For my purposes, I look at what is called "the policymakers within the White House," a term that the Office of Policy Development has internally developed. The senior policymakers are in the White House. The people with the title of special assistant and deputy assistant are in the Old Executive Office Building. The increase in staff members actually began with Richard Nixon. We are talking about a very small staff of six people who were on the Urban Affairs Council, and two assistants to Arthur Burns, who managed economic policy in the White House.

When John Ehrlichman took over, he began to use what is called "the detail" among White House staffs—people brought in from the departments to work for the White House. You are never really sure how many people are in the White House because it depends on how astute they are in bringing in detailees. If you look only at the numbers that are given to us from the budget of the White House staff for senior policymakers, this practice began to emerge under Nixon and the numbers moved up to about 20. At the height of Ehrlichman, he had about 45 staff members for domestic policy-making. Carter brought that number down, but at the end of the Reagan administration the number was up to 91. There were 70 staff members in the Bush administration, and Clinton is trying to further reduce that number. In 1989 the number of staff members peaked.

QUESTION: You have described several presidential styles and methods of policy-making, but you have not told us what you think of them in terms of governance. The presidential models contain some assumptions about Congress, the bureaucracy, political parties, and other things. On the matter of governance, what do you see in the long run?

MS. WARSHAW: One of the problems that emerges from a centralized policy-making system—that is one where the White House has enormous control—is that the departments' function as equalizer is diminished.   Within the departments you have the constituents' viewpoint, the public viewpoint, and the legislative needs, and policies developed in the departments really are policies that satisfy as many of those political blocs as possible. A White House-based system is developed by people in a vacuum. These policies meet the president's political needs but may not meet the political needs of all of the other disparate groups.

Reagan was able to bring the departments into the policy process. The White House staff would say to the Cabinet officers, "This is where we want to take these policies." They did not develop policies; they simply set a broad agenda showing the direction in which they wished to go. They went to the departments, let them work it out among their natural constituents, brought it back to the working groups, and then repeated this interaction. This procedure met the established criteria and tried to reduce gridlock, although there will always be gridlock. Gridlock is built into our institutional framework, but you can mitigate it. Reagan was quite successful at mitigating that gridlock.

QUESTION: Doesn't a president really have to start with votes? Reagan and FDR could have had any Cabinet they wanted. If you do not have enough votes and then you try to appoint only men, contemporaries, and conservatives, however, the media and Congress will take you apart.

MS. WARSHAW: I would argue that the American public wants to see that the mandate on which they elected their president is accomplished. They are less concerned with the blueprint of people surrounding the president than the successful initiation, implementation, and pursuance of a legislative package containing a series of programs the elected person is expected to advance. The American public elected Ronald Reagan to do several things: to reduce the federal budget, reduce the federal work force, increase the responsibility of states in the policy-making process, and reduce taxes. He accomplished all he had laid out. The American public wants to see the fruition of that mandate.

I would argue that the more people you have around you who are absolutely attuned to accomplishing your mandate rather than pursuing a series of departmentally preferred policies, the more respect and thus votes you will receive from the American public. Ronald Reagan was in office with a very clear agenda, so it was much easier for him to surround himself with people who agreed with that agenda than it was for George Bush, who did not have a clear agenda.

Bill Clinton was elected because the public wanted change, but it is very difficult to effect change without specifics. I believe national health care was Jim Carville's idea, which came out of nowhere in the Harris Wofford-Dick Thornburgh Senate race because they needed an issue. Bill Clinton was not wed to national health care until Jim Carville said, "Let's go with it."

The trouble with the Bush administration and the Clinton administration is that it is difficult to surround yourself with people with a shared vision and a shared agenda if you do not have a clear-cut agenda in the first place. Presidents also need to narrow their objectives to four or five very clear items that can be dealt with during the course of the administration. One of Bill Clinton's objectives early in the election was to bring gays into the military. That issue is very divisive, and as any student of the presidency would tell him, don't begin your presidency with a divisive issue because you have only four years—three in reality because one year is spent campaigning—to get your agenda before the public. You must have a narrow agenda, and to wage your battles on a divisive issue is political suicide.

QUESTION: I am impressed by your comments about the Reagan administration. My question has to do with the connection between governance, methodology, and political philosophies. I judge from what you say that a fairly uniform political philosophy was necessary in order to make the Reagan governance successful in achieving its objectives. Would you hold the same view with respect to Mr. Clinton, who was elected with 43 percent of the public vote, indicating that there was a wide scattering of political belief, whereas in Reagan's elections, the choices were somewhat less scattered?

MS. WARSHAW: When we elect a president, we are electing the most powerful person in the world—not just in the United States, but in the world today. We are electing a leader, and the key to that leadership is having a vision and an agenda for this country. If you do not agree with that vision, just throw the man or woman out in four years. That person has hopefully told you what he or she hopes to do for this country and what the agenda is. Then that person moves on with his or her vision, and that is what leadership is about.

NARRATOR: Do you think Donald Regan, Bill Casey, Ollie North, and Jim Baker shared Reagan's philosophy? Regan has said his problem for the first term was that in the beginning, he could never get through the California mafia. According to Regan, they blocked him at every point, and he had to find out what Reagan thought about economic policy by reading the newspapers.

Bill Casey and Ollie North seemed to operate in an orbit of their own. Is Jim Baker a possible exception in that his political philosophy may have been more closely associated with George Bush? What does that do to the concept? Does it modify it, or is it just an exception?

MS. WARSHAW: I think Donald Regan, as you pointed out, was not part of the inner circle. He didn't last very long. When Martin Anderson was director of the White House policy-making apparatus, he tightly controlled what Regan did in policy-making.

With regard to the Iran-contra situation, I would argue that Ronald Reagan clearly knew what was going on and that what these people were doing fit exactly in the mold about which I was talking. They were working to fulfill the Regan agenda. Reagan had said in no uncertain terms, "This is what I want to do in Nicaragua. This is what I want to do to support democracy. I want to support freedom fighters." They were implementing what he had said over and over again.

Jim Baker, in my opinion, is a political realist. Ed Meese was absolutely wedded to the Reagan political doctrine. Michael Deaver was not as wedded to the Reagan political doctrine, but was absolutely personally loyal to Reagan. Whatever Ronald Reagan wanted was fine with him.

Jim Baker came in as the political realist, and he realized his career was going to be enhanced by being part of this White House. He was perfectly willing to fine-tune his political objectives to meet those of the President. If you read any of the correspondence, you know that Jim Baker never argued against anything. He goes along with everyone else. There appear to be few instances where Jim Baker stood up and tried to bring the agenda in another direction.

QUESTION: Would you define a mandate? Does the election of a president become a mandate?

MS. WARSHAW: The mandate is that you have elected a president to do essentially whatever he wants to do at that point. He is the victor, as in a war, and the victor can therefore move forward based on what he's told the public. He refines what he has told the public, and then tries to accomplish those goals. A mandate is simply winning; it is not a matter of degrees. In presidential elections, someone wins and one or more people lose. The person who wins is now the president. He takes over the leadership of this country and moves it in his direction as best he can.

COMMENT: I think it is important and astounding that Reagan did not have more opposition to his vision. It seems to me that in addition to the way he organized his White House, one of the ways he deflected opposition was through his incredible control of the media. Every morning the Reagan White House put out their line and made sure it was what the media brought to the public.

MS. WARSHAW: The job of the White House press is very difficult. They have deadlines to meet, and every morning at 8:00 a.m. the approximately 1,200 people with press badges get into the White House to hear the babble that comes from the White House press secretary. Most of these people have a deadline for a radio show, newspaper, TV news, or whatever. They have to show something and do something. A skilled White House press office will give these people as much information as they possibly can on something relatively interesting. The skill of Larry Speakes and David Gergen (when he was the communications director) was that they pounded out unbelievable amounts of information for these people, and they controlled what got on the evening news. So when we talk about control of information, in large part we are talking about the ability to give the information directly to the press and keep them from going out on their own.

NARRATOR: Mr. Brownell was certainly right in his praise for Professor Warshaw's knowledge and abilities. We thank you very much for this interesting, scholarly, and informative presentation.

CHAPTER 6

POLICY INITIATIVES IN THE REAGAN ADMINISTRATION: COMMERCE*

C. WILLIAM VERITY

THE SECRETARY OF COMMERCE
WASHINGTON, D.C. 20230

January 6, 1989

Honorable Kenneth M. Duberstein
Chief of Staff to the President
The White House
Washington, D.C. 20500

Dear Ken,

This report recounts for you and the President results of initiatives you asked that we establish last spring in order to help make the last year of his Administration his proudest.

We listed 23 initiatives to you in a letter dated August 9, 1988. Since then we have added two more. A summary report on each is given below. Donna Tuttle and I, and the Commerce Department management, professional and career employees, are proud of these achievements.

Published by permission of C. William Verity.

1.   *Export Now*

This Government/private sector initiative encourages small- and medium-size companies to enter exporting.   The President's Advisory Committee on Exports will meet and present to me its report to the President on January 11.   I consider this one of Commerce's most successful programs. Seventy thousand companies started exporting in 1988.   And when the figures are in, we estimate that the U.S. trade deficit will have fallen in 1988 by nearly 20 percent—from $170 billion to $135 billion—and exports reached an all time level of $325 billion.

2.   *The Malcolm Baldrige National Quality Award*

This program, intended to recognize quality, excellence and promote greater quality awareness on the part of U.S. firms, got off to a good start with presentation of the first Awards by the President on November 14. It can do much in the years ahead to help our market position, competitiveness, and standard of living. Quality is the key to the future.   There is tremendous interest in this project in the private sector, as evidenced by the Quality Award Foundation raising $10 million to endow the Award.

3.   *Market Japan—with America's Best*

Our most difficult problems with Japan are their barriers to our exports.   This program seeks to open the Japanese distribution system so that U.S. companies can get more goods on the shelves in Japanese stores.   Twenty-five companies participated in the Presidential Mission sponsored by Minister Tamura of MITI and the Commerce Department. All are now meeting with success in getting their products into Japan at prices competitive to Japanese products. This program offers many possibilities for the future.

4.   *Europe 1992*

The Department of Commerce has geared itself to help America be ready to deal with the European Common Market when its new trade structure begins operating. The Department has established a highly knowledgeable bureau on EC 1992. We are in daily contact with Brussels, EC headquarters, and are providing information about EC 1992 to the private sector and to other Departments of government. We are working closely with State, Treasury, and USTR.

5. Coastal Environmental Quality Initiatives

One of our most pressing environmental problems and opportunities centers on our coastal areas. The Department's National Oceanic and Atmospheric Administration (NOAA) has pulled together a program covering research, problem diagnosis, forecasting and recommendations for action by other Federal agencies such as the Corps of Engineers and has forwarded the program to OMB for consideration. In an action related to this subject, a new Center for Ocean Analysis and Prediction was dedicated in Monterey, California, in October 1988.

6. Sludge Disposal Alternatives

NOAA has instituted a program, now well underway, for disposal of sludge (including compacted garbage) underneath the Continental Shelf. A trial disposal program has been funded with first results to be reported in 1989.

7. Three Secretaries' Education Initiative (Recognition that an educated workplace is key to our world competitiveness)

Under the leadership of the Secretaries of Labor, Education and Commerce, this is a joint program involving business, labor groups, education and government to build a quality work force in the United States. This program has moved exceptionally well, promoting partnerships between business and education at the local level aimed at upgrading the standards in the local school system so students will qualify for jobs upon graduation. Publications have been distributed and many such partnerships have been formed throughout the country.

8. Commercial Space Program/CDSF

On this one, we have not been successful. In February 1988, the President issued a 15-Point Commercial Space Initiative including a directive that NASA issue an RFP for a CDSF. We attempted to issue a request for proposal for this facility but were outmaneuvered by NASA, and then Congress. Just this week, NASA released an RFI to assess industry interest. It is an issue that should be addressed early on by the Bush Administration.

A speech on the need for furthering the commercialization of space will be delivered by the Secretary of Commerce on January 10 in Washington.

9.　Science and Technology Administration

The President signed legislation in early November creating an Under Secretary for Technology. The mission of this function is to provide a focus for Technology in the Commerce Department. U.S. competitiveness depends upon the ability of the private sector to commercialize technology. The Under Secretary, working with the Science Advisor in the White House and with technology administrators in other branches of the Government, can facilitate industry/government relationships.

10.　Government 2000

The Commerce Department recommended long-term goals and policy directions for the Government in the year 2000. We submitted this program to OMB and are in the process of revising and condensing the report for submission to the new Secretary of Commerce.

11.　Manufacturing Technology Centers

These Centers were authorized by the Trade Bill and funded by the 1988 Appropriations Act, calling for the establishment in 1988 of the first three such manufacturing centers to accelerate the commercial development and application of new technology. Three centers were selected by the National Institute of Standards and Technology and were announced at a ceremony in the Commerce Department on December 20. Members of Congress, the business community, the press, and officials from the three regions, New York, Ohio, and South Carolina, attended.

12. *Superconductivity Research*

As part of the President's superconductivity initiative, the National Institute of Standards and Technology is expanding its advanced research program through a new center for superconducting research in Boulder, Colorado. This will facilitate private sector industrial research on one of the great breakthroughs of this century. The research center will be opened in Boulder, Colorado, in January 1989.

13. *Antitrust Revamp*

We have been working with Attorney General Thornburgh on ways to revamp the antitrust laws so that American companies can cooperate in the research, development and production of new high technology products and services. An opening shot was joint Op/Ed articles by the Attorney General and myself in the December 27 Wall Street Journal. A press event will follow to help set the stage for encouraging legislation in the 101st Congress to implement this initiative.

14. *Commercial Information Management Systems*

This program will provide information needed by our U.S. and Foreign Commercial Service offices throughout the world to help U.S. exporters. We expected it to come on line in 1988 but decided to change the mission for CIMS. Working with others in Commerce and elsewhere in the Federal Government, it will provide a new system for getting appropriate and adequate international trade information to our U.S. District Offices and Foreign Commercial Service offices. CIMS will provide a warehouse of information where users can hook up with the new national information service.

15. *High-Definition Television (HDTV)*

The Department is working with and through an advisory group established last summer. The private sector companies involved with the advisory board are making progress in coming up with a recommendation as to how the United States can compete—and then excel in this emerging new technology. The advisory committee's report is due January 18.

16. *1990 Census*

The Census Bureau is on target with each step being completed as planned. The pre-list field work was completed in December. A dress rehearsal census was staged March 1988 in St. Louis and portions of Missouri and the State of Washington. An evaluation of the dress rehearsal is due in April 1989. At year's end we announced a major promotional tie-in of the 1990 Census in conjunction with the National Association of Broadcasters.

17. *Automated Patent System*

Automating the Patent System has been a major project of the Commerce Department over the last eight years. We straightened out some management problems, and in November we cut a ribbon inaugurating the new technology which will, within two years, bring all patents into an automated, computerized system.

18. *Bank Community Development Corporation*

In the spirit of the Administration's position on phasing out the Economic Development Administration, Assistant Secretary Swindle has developed an innovative plan for local financing rather than Federal grants for developing purposes in communities. Creation of the Community Development Corporations was the subject of a news conference on January 5. At the Commerce Department six pilot programs were announced at that time.

19. *Economic Development Initiative in the Pacific Islands*

On another front, the EDA Assistant Secretary has worked on making grants to Pacific Island nations, our former territories, which will help them develop their countries and at the same time create closer ties with the United States.

20. *Drug-Free Workplace*

Secretary McLaughlin and I participated in a landmark event during 1988 to further the anti-drug program. It focused on a program sponsored by the CSX Corporation and several of its labor unions. Commerce has put together, and has readily available, a program to mobilize industry throughout the country to work towards a drug-free workplace. We have compiled names of business chief executives to serve on the Secretarial Advisory Board of Drug-Free America. This information will be made available to the new administration.

21. *Telecom 2000*

A report by our National Telecommunication and Information Administration describes what needs to be done to ensure that the United States takes full advantage of new telecommunications technology. The report will be used by Federal agencies to guide priorities in policy development in the near term and up to the year 2000.

22. *Privatization Initiative*

We have identified 30 projects which have been submitted to OMB for A-76 reviews. We are putting into effect programs for contracting-out National Technical Information Service sales and distribution functions.

23. *Child Day Care Center*

We cut the ribbon for the new Child Day Care Center on December 20. Open for business in early January, it will be one of the best such centers in Washington. Commerce employees have contributed to a scholarship fund which will provide help for disadvantaged families who cannot afford the full cost of the Center.

24. *Office of Private Sector Initiatives*

In November, we opened an Office of Private Sector Initiatives under the leadership of Dan Sullivan. He has been working closely with the White House in order to promote Administration programs and to supplement White House activities in this important area.

25. *Statistics*

While our economic statistics are much better than our critics contend, they are not as good as they should be. We have sought and obtained from OMB funding in the new budget for a major improvement in several important statistical series, including some major components of the GNP.

Sincerely,

C. William Verity

cc: Honorable Nancy Risque

CHAPTER 7

THE REAGAN PRESIDENCY AND HEALTH CARE IN THE UNITED STATES*

OTIS R. BOWEN

NARRATOR: If Thomas Jefferson were here today he would have approved of the public service that Otis Bowen has given his country at the local, state, and national levels. He has been elected county coroner (1952-1956) and has served as a member of the Indiana House of Representatives (1956-1958, 1960-1972), where he performed the roles of both minority leader (1965-1967) and Speaker of the House (1967-1972). He also served as vice chairman and chairman of Indiana's Legislative Council (1967-1968, 1970-1972). In 1973, Otis Bowen was elected governor of Indiana and served in that capacity until 1981. He was also elected chairman of all three major governors' conferences—the Midwest Governors' Conference, the Republican Governors' Conference, and the National Governors' Conference.

Otis Bowen's public service at the national level is equally impressive. During the Reagan administration, he served as the secretary of health and human services, was a member of both President Ford's Commission on Science and Technology and the Commission on Federalism, and chaired an important advisory committee on Social Security that was established during the Reagan administration. We look forward to his contribution to the Miller Center's Reagan oral history.

Presented in a Forum at the Miller Center of Public Affairs on 31 August 1992.

GOVERNOR BOWEN: I was elected to my first political office—that of county coroner—in 1952. I held that office until 1956, when I became a member of the Indiana House of Representatives. With four children to feed and educate, I was able to serve as a legislator only because the legislature then met only 61 calendar days every two years, allowing me to maintain my medical practice.

Being a legislator at that time was also expensive because I had to bear my own campaign expenses and live away from home, which meant eating in restaurants and staying in hotels. Back then I never heard of a fund-raiser, whereas now there is a fund-raiser for everything. Nevertheless, now that the legislature meets every year and for longer sessions, I probably would not have had the means to serve in the legislature under the present times.

I had been a representative for 14 years when I became governor of Indiana in 1973. After serving two terms as governor, I took a position at Indiana University as professor of family medicine, which was the position I was holding when the White House called with the request that I become President Reagan's secretary of health and human services.

Up to that point, my public service had already marked a number of "firsts." I was the first Speaker of the House to serve three terms, the first governor ever to serve two successive four-year terms in Indiana, and the first physician to serve as governor. On 13 December 1985, I also became the first physician ever to serve as secretary of health and human services, which seems unusual to me because it strikes me that the nature of the job should require that it always be held by a physician. I also served the longest of all of the secretaries of health and human services who preceded me. The average length of time that secretaries had served before me was two years; I served until 19 January 1989, a little over three years. I had wanted to leave earlier, but I had told the President that I would wait until he found a replacement. In the end, no replacement was found, and the position was vacant for about three months.

I feel compelled to mention that President Reagan's outgoing secretaries were all treated rather poorly by the incoming Bush administration. President Bush was inaugurated on 19 January 1989; I received the call on the afternoon of 18 January to vacate my office by noon the next day. Moreover, members of the Reagan administration were given terrible seats at the inauguration. The seats were so bad that we could not see who was on the podium. I do not think President Bush was responsible; he likely did not know of these arrangements. Rather, I suspect that John Sununu is the one to blame. As the new chief of staff, Sununu wanted a quick, easy break and thus wanted to replace all of the Reagan people with Bush people as soon as possible.

I was named President Reagan's secretary of health and human services for a number of reasons. First, my previous relationship with Dan Quayle, who sponsored my name, was instrumental to my nomination. When I was governor and before he became a successful congressman and senator, Quayle had worked for me for a couple of years. Later, when my gubernatorial term expired and I was expected to run for the Senate, Quayle was willing to defer to me, even though he wanted to run for the Senate himself. When I did not run due to my wife's serious illness and subsequent death, Quayle had buttons printed that said "If not Bowen, then Quayle!"

A second reason for my being named secretary of health and human services was my acquaintance with Ronald Reagan. Both he and I had served overlapping terms as governors of our respective states and had become acquainted at the various governors' conferences. A third reason was probably political, as Indiana had overwhelmingly supported President Reagan in both 1980 and 1984. Finally, my governmental and medical background provided reasonable qualifications for the position of secretary.

Before being offered the job, I remember telling my medical colleagues that I would never want the job of secretary of health and human services because so much controversy and so many problems are attached to the office and it is such a huge department. When the president places a personal call to make a request of a person, however, it is difficult to say no.

There was a whirlwind of activity after the President called me in November. I had to be in Washington for his announcement of my nomination and for pictures. I went back and forth between Washington and Indianapolis several times in the few weeks before the Senate confirmation hearings. I had to prepare for those hearings and make the necessary courtesy calls on the various senators and congressmen who would confirm or reject my nomination.

My position as a secretary was just as awesome as I had expected it to be. In 1989 Health and Human Services (HHS) had a budget of $425 billion and employed about 120,000 people from all over the world. It had over 300 separate programs and too many bosses to count—some from Congress, some from the White House, and some from the Budget Office. A total of 23 congressional oversight committees were assigned to the various programs administered by HHS. HHS was kept very busy, running back and forth between the department and the Hill, trying to protect what it had done and trying to explain what it had not done.

There were also many organizations from all over the United States dealing with both broad and specific domestic issues. HHS was composed of many departments, and each of those had several subdepartments. The main ones were the Social Security Administration and the Public Health Service, including the Surgeon General's Office. Incidentally, C. Everett Koop is an enlightened and a great fellow. Even though he served under me, I gave him a great deal of discretion because he was quotable and the news media liked him. He was very effective at getting out a message. For that reason *Every Door*, the AIDS publication, was published under his name. I thought that his name would encourage more people to read it than otherwise would have.

Other big departments under Health and Human Services include the National Institutes of Health; the Centers for Disease Control; the Food and Drug Administration; the Alcohol, Drug Abuse, and Mental Health Administration; Health Resources and Services Administration; Administration for Native Americans; Health Care Financing Administration; and Medicare and Medicaid.

In terms of time and harassment, the biggest problems handled by HHS while I was secretary were AIDS, food and drug tampering—people were injecting cyanide into oranges, grapes, and over-the-counter drugs—abortion, fetal-tissue research, and animal rights. The Office of Management and Budget (OMB), personnel associated with the White House budget, oversight committees, and the pet projects of individual congressmen also took a good deal of the department personnel's time and attention.

HHS also had to respond to many outside organizations, such as the Right to Life; Choice; Planned Parenthood; PETA (People for the Ethical Treatment of Animals), the very vocal animal rights group; AIDS groups; and the homeless, especially Mitch Snyder, who was a champion for the homeless in Washington. There is also AARP and various health provider associations such as the American Medical Association, insurance companies, hospitals, HMOs, and organizations for specific diseases such as arthritis, diabetes, heart, lung, head injury, pediatrics, and others. All of these groups wanted appointments with the HHS secretary, and it was impossible to be so many places at one time.

The pressure for change in health care is constant and comes from every possible source—patients, providers, insurers, businesses, labor, and government at all levels. New techniques, new procedures, changing demographics, and the constant emergence of new players mean that there will always be pressure for health care reform. Over the last 30 years, five significant enactments have prompted major changes in policy: the establishment of Medicare, Medicaid, and DRGs, the Medicare Catastrophic Coverage Act of 1988, and then its repeal in 1989.

The goals of government, the American people, and health care providers are all essentially the same; these groups just disagree about the means by which to achieve good health care. They all want quality care and access to care, and they want it at an affordable price. They are miles apart from one another, however, when it comes to developing or implementing a plan to meet those goals.

The American people, including those in government and elected office, no longer have as high a regard for the medical profession as they once did. The perception that people have of physicians as a group, the pharmaceutical industry, and hospitals is that they are getting rich at the expense of sick people. That attitude seems to be prevalent in government now as well.

The desire to provide quality care is additionally complicated by the need to balance the federal budget. Congress is torn between the overwhelming and all-consuming issue of the budget and the desire to provide for America's health needs, which they know will add some cost to government. Nevertheless, it seems that budget is driving policy rather than policy driving budget in the health care area. HHS's efforts to pass the Medicare Catastrophic Coverage Bill provide a good example of the tensions and problems encountered.

As secretary of health and human services, I had tremendous responsibility but very little authority, which makes it difficult to accomplish much. I could not even make a speech without someone from the Office of Management and Budget and the White House staff reading and editing it. That example demonstrates how closely the administration guarded what its secretaries were saying.

My responsibilities as secretary included keeping the President apprised of the health and welfare of the American people and ensuring that adequate research was being done in those areas where research was needed but which private research had not addressed. A third major responsibility that I had as secretary of health and human services was to look after the income security of the poor, the disabled, and the elderly.

Senior citizens have two big worries—their health and their finances, and they worry about which one will run out first. Programs are greatly needed that will give peace of mind to the people by providing some insurance against the loss of their life savings due to some catastrophic illness.

Over the next generation, the group of people between the ages of 65 and 74 will increase by 80 percent. The group consisting of those between the ages of 74 and 85 will experience a 200 percent increase, and the group of those people above the age of 85 will increase 280 percent. Currently, 25,000 people living in the United States are over the age of 100. These elderly people are frail and require considerable care.

Given increased longevity and current age eligibility requirements, three generations of people are already drawing funds from Medicare and Social Security at the same time. Consequently, only one or two generations at most are paying into the program. As people live longer, resulting in greater numbers of the aged, the problems involved in providing adequate care to people is going to get worse instead of better.

Protecting the patient in instances of catastrophic illnesses was therefore a popular idea with Congress. The administration, however, was fearful due to the great cost involved. Because of the budget deficit, it was a foregone conclusion that any new program to protect the elderly against those losses would have to be cost-neutral to the government and that those who benefited from it would have to pay. That assumption was reasonable and understandable.

The President was sympathetic to the need for such a program, and in his 1986 State of the Union Address he charged me with a specific responsibility. "I am directing the secretary of health and human services, Dr. Otis Bowen," he said, "to report to me by year's end with recommendations on how the private sector and government can work together to address the problems of afford-able insurance for those whose life savings would otherwise be threatened when catastrophic illness strikes." The President followed the public address with a personal letter to me restating the charges:

> The issue has concerned me for many years. I know of your proposal suggesting an answer to catastrophic illness expenses not covered by the current Medicare program. This has certainly helped to focus public and congressional attention to the important issue. Your efforts should include, but not be limited to, examining situations faced by Medicare beneficiaries as well as people of all age groupings, income, and employment status. You should look at what the private sector and the levels of government are doing to address the problems and examine current federal activities from tax policy that affects private health insurance to financing programs, such as Medicare, Medicaid, and veterans' health benefits. You should make recommendations through the Domestic Policy Council process on further steps, if any, that are warranted by the private sector, states, local government, and the federal government.
>
> I have no preconceived notions about what the right answer should be. I truly appreciate your willingness to take on this major issue so early in your tenure. I look forward to receiving the plan in December of this year containing recom-mendations that I can study in order to determine actions that can be taken in 1987 toward lifting a great financial burden from the backs of many citizens.
>
> Sincerely Yours,
> Ronald Reagan

My marching orders were thus pretty explicit. The President asked for recommendations—something that I had to remind and re-remind the members of the Domestic Policy Council (DPC) several times, once even in front of the President at the Cabinet meeting where it was presented, discussed, and debated.

After the President's directive, I organized the HHS study by creating an executive advisory committee, which was composed of senior members of my staff and chaired by my chief of staff, Tom Burke. I also created three technical working groups within the department, each of which would focus its attention on just one segment of the study.

The three segments of the study were the catastrophic health expenses of the general population, the catastrophic health expenses of Medicare beneficiaries, and long-term care. This report gave extensive coverage to the first segment—that is, the catastrophic health expenses of the general population, which is mainly those below the age of 65. This group, however, received very little attention from the administration. The second segment, Medicare beneficiaries, received the attention of Congress, and it was this group that Congress addressed. The third segment, long-term care, was also the subject of extensive study by HHS, but it received little attention.

In addition to these departmental working groups, I also created a private-public sector advisory committee on catastrophic illness whose purpose was to seek private sector input on how the private sector and government could work together to address the problem of affordable insurance for catastrophic illnesses. This group held five or six meetings at various places throughout the country.

To get the report to the President by the target date of 15 December, the study and recommendations had to be put before the Domestic Policy Council by 15 September. Though HHS met the preparation deadlines, the report was not received by the Domestic Policy Council until 19 November 1986.

The Domestic Council was one of three councils through which issues came before the President. The other two were the National Security Council, whose membership is limited to appropriate Cabinet members and military members, and the Economic Security Council. Although Health and Human Services was the big player in the Domestic Policy Council, the council was chaired by Attorney General Edwin Meese. Although he disagreed with the need for a program protecting people against catastrophic illness, he nevertheless was the one who organized the agenda, conducted the meetings, and appointed subcommittees. Led by Edwin Meese, Treasury Undersecretary Beryl Sprinkel, Jim Miller, the director of the Office of Management and Budget, and Secretary of Interior Donald P. Hodel, the opposition was instant and intense.

At first, I had no visible support from any Cabinet member. Not until later did I receive support from Secretary of Labor Bill Brock and Secretary of Defense Caspar Weinberger. Their previous experiences, both political and public, gave them insight into people's needs and wants. Weinberger had served as HHS secretary for a time, and Brock was a former senator. Of all of the Cabinet members, he and I were the only two who had been the subjects of political campaigns and elections. President Reagan's former political experience as governor similarly made him much more aware and sensitive to people's needs. All of the other Cabinet members were quietly opposed to the program. Strong opposition would also come from groups like the Heritage Foundation and the Chamber of Commerce.

The opposing forces reminded me of something F. M. Cornford wrote in his book *Microcosmographia Academica* (1970). In it, he wrote, "The principle of the dangerous precedent is that you should not now do any or do an admittedly right action for fear that you or your equally timid successor should not have the courage to do right in some future time. . . . Every public action which is not customary either is wrong, or if it is right, is a dangerous precedent. It follows that nothing should be done for the first time!" My experience at HHS reminds me of these words.

HHS had been careful about not letting its study and report leak out to the public, but once it was before the Domestic Policy Council, it could no longer be kept quiet because the DPC was a great source of leaks of this kind. For this reason, the DPC reluctantly approved my scheduling of a news conference for the next morning. At that news conference, I announced what I had presented but was careful to emphasize that the results were from my study and that neither the DPC nor the President had endorsed any part of it.

Six DPC meetings were held, three of them with the President in which my recommendations were discussed. Were it not for my appeal to the secretary of the Cabinet and the secretary of DPC, who discussed it with Chief of Staff Don Regan, I may never have had the opportunity to show the President my findings. I had to remind them of the President's directive and order to me requesting that I present recommendations to him.

Meese and others merely wanted three or four options presented without recommendations. They even created a few options of their own to present, and Meese, the chairman of the DPC, would not call on me at meetings with the President. Despite his efforts to the contrary, however, I made certain that I had the opportunity to debate the recommendations with them before the President at two of those meetings. Nine days after the final meeting with the President in which he said he would make a decision after reviewing the materials, I was summoned to the White House to explain the plan for covering catastrophic illnesses. The President had given his blessing to my plan.

The opposing forces, however, had settled on a voucher system, and the telling blow came when I attempted to trace the path of the voucher. The voucher would first go to patient, who would then send money to his or her chosen insurance company. The money would then be sent to the patient for payment to the doctors and/or hospital. Part of the difficulty of such a plan was the assumption that a 95-year old patient would be able to make necessary contacts with the insurance company.

After approving the plan, the President requested that HHS prepare legislation to present to Congress, which was completed by 16 February 1987. The legislation then had to go to OMB for approval, but since the President had spoken, it could no longer be blocked. Nevertheless, opponents did try to shape the legislation to their liking as it progressed through Congress.

The bill was introduced in the House of Representatives on 24 February 1987 with 38 co-sponsors. It was introduced in the Senate with 16 co-sponsors. Many hours of Senate and House committee hearings followed at which I had to testify and try to answer their questions. On 1 July 1987, the bill was voted out of the House Committee on Energy and Commerce, which handled HHS problems. On 22 July 1987, it passed the House by 302 votes to 127. The House bill was then sent to the Senate on 24 July, where the Senate's recent bill was incorporated into the House bill. On 27 October, after three months of hearings, it passed the Senate by 86 votes to 11. The House's disagreements with the Senate's amendments, however, caused the bill to be referred to a conference committee on 9 December 1987. Because the Senate did not appoint their conferees until 2 February, conference meetings were not called until 16 March 1988—five months after the Senate passed the bill. I am quite sure that members of the administration, DPC, and others opposed to the plan were responsible for the delay and were trying to scuttle it or change it.

Between 16 March and 25 May, the conference committee met many times. At the committee's invitation, I was called to meet with the conferees to advocate the administration's position. The conferees then released the approved and amended version of the bill. On 2 June 1988, a year after the target-date set by the President in his State of the Union message, the House passed the conference committee report by 328 votes to 72, and on 8 June 1988, the Senate passed it 86 to 11. On 1 July 1988, the President signed the legislation in the Rose Garden with the congressmen who had been influential in the bill's passage and me in attendance.

That moment was a proud one for me, and many acknowledged and thanked me for my efforts. The 5 July 1988 publication of the National Health Council reported: "Upon achieving final compromise on the unprecedented legislation, House and Senate conferees rose and gave Bowen a standing round of applause to show their appreciation." I also received personal letters of thanks from Senator Lloyd Bentsen, the chairman of the Senate's Finance Committee of the Senate, and President Reagan. Senator Bentsen wrote:

Dear Mr. Secretary:

The vision and perseverance, which you've brought to the development of the Medicare Catastrophic Coverage Act of 1988, were invaluable. Yours was a difficult role, executed brilliantly and with sensitivity to the needs of a frail and vulnerable population of Americans. I want you to know that I consider it a privilege to have worked side by side with you in bringing this legislation to fruition.

With warm regards,
Lloyd Bentsen

Then on 14 October 1988, I received a letter from the President that said:

Dear Otis,

It was a pleasure for me to have you present at the signing for HR 2470, the Medicare Catastrophic Coverage Act of 1988, in the Rose Garden. This historic legislation responds to my State of the Union Address to Congress, January 27, 1986, calling for help to free the elderly from the fear of catastrophic illness. It will help remove a terrible threat from the lives of elderly and disabled Americans the threat of an illness requiring acute care that could wipe out the savings of an entire lifetime.

To express my appreciation for your leadership on behalf of this bill, it is my pleasure to present you with the enclosed pen I used to sign the bill into law.

Sincerely,
Ronald Reagan

Altogether, it took two-and-a-half years—from the day of my Senate confirmation hearings in December 1985 until the day the President signed the bill in July 1988—for the bill to become law. It was repealed in 1989.

The 1988 Medicare Catastrophic Coverage Act covered all hospital bills after the patient paid for the first day of coverage and capped on the first day's coverage at $560. The act increased skilled nursing home care to 150 days with less co-payment cost to the patient per day. Respite care was increased to 80 hours, and home health care was increased to 38 days. The act also included mammography. For physician coverage, after the patient paid out-of-pocket expenses of $1,370 (using the existing formula of the patient paying the first $75 plus 20 percent of the allowed Medicare coverage), Medicare would pay the remainder of those expenses that Medicare then covered. These arrangements helped to prevent spousal impoverishment. Beginning in 1991, payment of drugs after a $650 deductible would also be covered. In the first year, Medicare would pay 50 percent of that cost; the second year, 60 percent; and the third year, 80 percent.

The act also made some changes in Medicaid that increased the eligibility of pregnant women and children. It was also indexed for inflation. All beneficiaries would pay at least $4 a month, but fees would be based on a graduated scale, with the poor paying no more and those financially better off paying more but with an upper limit of $800 per year. With this bill, the need for expensive "Medigap" coverage would therefore be questionable. One could still get "Medigap" insurance to cover that $2,000 at risk and whatever Medicare would not cover, such as glasses and dental care. To cover these costs, the upper 40 percent of the population were to help the lower 60 percent pay the bill. It would have been much more palatable to people if those numbers had been reversed.

The government's health care program has been compared to a patchwork quilt, with individual patches for the elderly, the poor, veterans, the military, and workers. The lawmakers over the years have tried to cover more and more Americans, but in 1989 that patchwork quilt began to unravel with the repeal of the Medicare Catastrophic Coverage Act. It was repealed for several reasons. First, well-to-do senior citizens raised opposition. Second, misinformation was received from Jimmy Roosevelt's group, Save Social Security, which intimated constantly that everyone would be paying $800 a year more. That allegation was far from the truth. Only those in the upper 5 percent—those people whose incomes equaled or exceeded $86,000 a year—would have been required to pay $800.

The silence of the Bush administration toward the act also contributed to its repeal. The administration did not do anything to defend it against some of the negative press it was receiving, such as *Time*'s cover that featured a 69-year-old lady draped over the hood of Dan Rostenkowski's car in his home district, complaining about the bill. Another reason for the act's repeal was that Congress added too many bells and whistles to it, making the act more expensive. Congress's formula for payment of the costs involved was also unsatisfactory. The AARP had backed every item that had been added to the act. Congress underestimated the strength and vocalness of well-to-do retirees. As Lynn Etheridge, a health consultant, said when the act was repealed, "We have discovered the higher income elderly are a fairly vocal group." Congress did apply two new and unprecedented principles to the act. First, Congress stipulated that the beneficiary pay the bill and second that those who were better off pay more with those less well off paying less.

In the end, the bill was complicated and went far beyond what was initially introduced. For example, the additional coverage of drugs was unnecessary, expensive, and would have been an administrative nightmare. I do not know how the country would have handled a program of 30 million people, determined when each one had reached their $650 deductible, and then what percentage each was to pay after those calculations. Every drugstore would have had to have a computer, and with people going to different drugstores for their medicines, administering that part of the program would have been a nightmare.

Several other points about the act are worth noting. First, Congress never should have added so many items to the original act. All of the additions were humane, compassionate, and desirable, but they added considerably to the overall cost. The idea behind the addition is much like the idea behind car insurance or fire insurance on one's home. People pay the premium but hope that it will not be a losing investment and that they will never have to fall back on that insurance, even though they have paid into it. The problem was that not many people saw the Catastrophic Coverage Act that way.

Second, Congress should never have repealed the act. It should have brought the act back and worked at it until people found it acceptable. All that Congress really had to do was cancel the additional drug coverage, which was the most expensive portion of the act.

Also, people over 65 have far more net worth than any other age group. In addition, the bill was a bargain with respect to cost because there was no physical exam, no preexisting conditions, no age limit, and no time limit that had to expire before a person was covered. In short, the "Medigap" cost should have gone down and may have even disappeared completely.

Too many senior citizens are overinsured with limited policies on specific diseases. Some older people have eight to 12 insurance policies—a separate one for cancer and others for different diseases or conditions—and they are paying big bills on all of them when many of the policies are unnecessary.

At the time of the repeal, beneficiaries were paying only 25 percent of the premium cost for doctor and outpatient care with tax revenues paying the rest. Moreover, with respect to hospital care, the 11 September 1989 issue of *Newsweek* reports that those retiring would on the average be getting back five times more benefits than they ever contributed. Future beneficiaries, however, are unlikely to receive as high a return on their Social Security investment. On average, individuals currently receive 25 times more in Social Security than they pay into the system. Consider, however, that it takes about one-and-a-half times as much money to take care of an 85-year-old's health than it does a for a person 65 years old and that the older one gets, the more expensive it becomes to care for them and the less able their children, who are also growing older, will be able to help them.

When Social Security first began, 16 people worked and paid into the system for every one person drawing from it. Today, however, only 3.4 people work and pay into the program for each person drawing from it. With people's ever-increasing longevity, the ratio will become narrower—3 to 1; 2½ to 1; 2 to 1— until the situation becomes impossible to handle. Unless something changes, the HHS budget can therefore only increase.

The age of eligibility is something that must be changed, but Congress cannot seem to make that move because it is political suicide. Congress did increase the age of eligibility but made it effective sometime in the distant future; that is, when all of the present members of Congress would be gone and none would be around to take the blame.

I suggested, although my suggestion was totally ignored by Congress, that the age of eligibility should be linked to the age of longevity so that it would be automatic. At least that way some of the Medicare costs could be reduced. Medicare currently spends about 30 percent of its funds on people who are in their last year of life. It spends 23 percent on those in the last six months of life and 11 percent on those in the last 40 days of life, which is the time when many heroic types of measures are taken, even though physicians know such measures are often futile.

In the United States there is much disparity in the quality of hospital care patients receive. From hospital to hospital differences can be seen in bedding or overbedding, admission rates, length of stays, the types of surgery performed, and so forth. A Boston-New Haven study made three or four years ago compared two good medical communities and found that one community performed a great number more hip replacements while the other community performed many more hysterectomies. Both were good, solid medical communities, yet they performed much different medical services.

Some outcome studies need to be made to determine the best treatment for specific conditions. Such a study would provide guidelines for physicians and others to evaluate the quality of care and whether certain procedures are necessary or not. A number of reasons exist for increasing medical costs. Certainly, there is enough blame to go around. First, the tremendous advances in diagnostic and therapeutic technology increase the cost. Moreover, each hospital always wants the newest and finest equipment for itself, even though a nearby hospital may have that same equipment. Each also wants to provide a wide selection of services. As a result, services are often duplicated by neighboring hospitals. Sometimes duplication even occurs within the same institution. More cooperation between hospitals in the same area is needed, and more specialization of certain services should occur to avoid duplication and reduce the cost of those services.

Second, physicians also contribute to rising medical costs because they dictate health care demands. Though they receive only 20 percent of the health care dollar, they control or prescribe most of the other 80 percent. Physicians have to practice defensive medicine. A neurosurgeon in Florida must pay a $200,000 annual premium for malpractice insurance. An obstetrician in Florida must pay around $80,000 a year for his malpractice premium. Consequently, family physicians have stopped delivering babies, and many obstetricians have quit doing so simply because the cost of their malpractice insurance is too high. Moreover, if physicians do not try everything possible, even procedures that might be minimally effective, they open themselves up to a potential lawsuit. This kind of defensive medicine therefore also contributes to high medical costs.

Third, insurers must also take the blame because of the blank checks they have given hospitals and physicians in the past. Employees and unions have demanded first-dollar coverage and have gotten it. Employers acquiesced to their demands.

Fourth, The changing demographics I mentioned earlier further contribute to rising costs. With people living longer now, more medical bills will be incurred.

Fifth, the government must also accept a considerable amount of the blame. It has allowed corporate tax breaks to employers for health insurance for their employees. The government also has not taxed employee benefits. These issues are arguable, but at the very least the government needs to discuss and debate them.

Also contributing to rising costs is the judicial system that has permitted excessive awards in malpractice claims, some of which have not been legitimate. If a person gets an elbow crushed in an accident, that person will end up with a stiff elbow no matter how many of the world's best orthopedic surgeons may have examined the elbow. Yet if the patient waves that elbow in front of a jury, he or she is apt to get a fairly good settlement. This kind of settlement is not right!

The government also contributes to rising medical costs with its huge paperwork requirements but also with its support of the tobacco industry, which causes 300,000 unnecessary deaths every year in addition to all of the nonfatal illnesses smoking causes.

Finally, one of the biggest reasons for the high cost of medical care is individual patients who live unhealthy lifestyles, practice unsafe sex, drink alcohol, take drugs, do not wear seat belts, and so forth.

QUESTION: Your discussion of the Medicare Catastrophic Coverage Act seems to highlight the unwillingness of the American public to make the necessary adjustments that would make health care in this country reasonably fair for everyone. Do you have any hope that this type of change can occur in this country?

GOVERNOR BOWEN: Congress will not enact anything anymore in the health care area until they have the consensus of every possible group that might gripe about it, which is unlikely. Higher medical costs and Congress's unwillingness to do anything about it means that a more difficult problem will have to be addressed later.

Ultimately, the United States may end up with national health insurance, a situation that is possible for three reasons. Over 30 million older people would vote for it. Labor unions would favor it. Even big companies such as General Motors are in favor of national health insurance because they have been unable to hold costs down and now want the government to step in and help them. The combination of old people, labor, and now some of the big companies is too much political clout for Congress to ignore.

The type of national health insurance that might ultimately became an actuality is debatable. Some people think that it might be like the Canadian example. One cannot criticize the Canadian system too much, given some of its statistics. For example, Canada's age of longevity is greater than ours and its infant mortality rate is less than ours. Canada, therefore, must be doing something right. On the other hand, Canadians who want or need high-tech treatment come to the United States for it. A couple of years ago Canada only had 11 or 12 places that performed cardiac surgery; the United States had 800. In short, the United States has too many, but Canada has too few.

I have also been told that some of the hospitals in Canada keep costs down by having patients bring their own soap, towels, sheets, and pillowcases.

QUESTION: Doesn't the Department of Health and Human Services present a nightmare, given its 23 oversight committees and the 130,000 people employed there? Nothing in the American people's experience indicates that a huge bureaucracy such as that department will be effective or efficient.

GOVERNOR BOWEN: The Medicare overhead is very little. When I first began at HHS, approximately 140,000 people worked there. When I left, employment figures were down to 115,000. I have found that those who served the department and the Medicare program were willing and devoted people.

The expense of running HHS was not out-of-line considering the mandates that Congress gave it. The 23 oversight committees exist to ensure that the department is complying with those mandates.

QUESTION: If people protested high hospital bills, would their complaints help keep costs down?

GOVERNOR BOWEN: Though I am supposed to be an expert on understanding medical bills, I found the bills that accumulated during my wife's two prolonged illnesses very confusing. There were so many codes—the doctor had a code; each procedure had a code, and so forth. At the time, however, I was in no mood to track down each of the items on my bill, so perhaps I lost the opportunity to make the health care industry more accountable. Other people or their family members who have been through an illness are probably also too mentally stressed to check bills closely and verify the many charges.

COMMENT: People can appeal to whoever supervises the particular medical program about their bill. For example, in Indiana one would appeal to an arm of the Blue Cross/Blue Shield insurance company. One could write a letter identifying areas of complaint of dissatisfaction and someone would look into it. The Medicare pamphlet for an area should identify the people who administer the program for that area.

NARRATOR: As consumers, we all appreciate Governor Bowen's very simple and direct presentation of a department and program that affects so many of us, and we are grateful for his contribution to our understanding of the functions of HHS.

III

THE
INTERNATIONAL ARENA

CHAPTER 8

REAGAN, BUSH, AND THE FUTURE OF INTERNATIONAL TRADE*

CLAYTON YEUTTER

NARRATOR: Clayton Yeutter is with Hogan & Hartson, one of the largest and oldest law firms in Washington, D.C. He deals especially with trade, food, and agricultural policy issues. Mr. Yeutter received a bachelor of science degree, J.D., and a doctorate from the University of Nebraska. He ranked first in his graduating class in the bachelor's and J.D. programs, and was named outstanding graduate student in agricultural economics during his doctoral program. He also distinguished himself by receiving seven honorary degrees from Georgetown University, the University of Nebraska, Clemson University, and other institutions.

Mr. Yeutter served as U.S. trade representative, a Cabinet post reporting directly to President Reagan. He was secretary of agriculture in the Bush administration, one of the largest departments with a budget of $50 billion and 100,000 employees. In 1991 he became chairman of the Republican National Committee. Before his service in government, he was president and chief executive officer of the Chicago Mercantile Exchange, dealing with a wide range of issues of great importance to the nation's economy. He held earlier positions as deputy special trade representative, assistant secretary of agriculture (in two separate positions), regional director of the Committee to Reelect President

---

*Presented in a Forum at the Miller Center of Public Affairs on 18 November 1994.

Nixon, and director of the University of Nebraska's mission in Colombia, a program dealing with agriculture and related subjects. He was also executive assistant to the governor of Nebraska and a faculty member of the Department of Agricultural Economics at the University of Nebraska. Very few people have had the opportunity to compare the Reagan and Bush administrations in quite the way that Secretary Yeutter has had. We look forward to his discussion of world trade and perhaps some comments on the recent election.

MR. YEUTTER: As a result of my having occupied high-level positions in both the Reagan and Bush administrations, I thought I would provide a comparative analysis of their approaches to governing the nation and dealing with world events during their administrations. I think there are some meaningful differences that might be worth exploring.

The old axiom is that there is a time and place for everything, and there may be a time and place for every person in this world as well. I believe that is true of the presidency: We need particular kinds of individuals to lead us at various junctures in the nation's history. I do not know whether it is fortune or luck or whether we Americans just have good instincts in a democratic society, but it seems that throughout our 200-plus years of history, we have done a good job of getting the right person in the right place at the right time in the presidency. We have not always got it right, but on the average, I would say Americans have done quite well. In comparing these two presidents, Ronald Reagan was certainly there in good times for the country, some of which were clearly attributable to him. George Bush was there in some bad times, many of which were *not* attributable to him. Historians can decide their places in history as time passes.

President Reagan first tried for the top slot in this nation in 1976, running unsuccessfully against Jerry Ford in the primary. That loss was probably one of the best things that ever happened to Ronald Reagan because in my judgment, 1977 would not have been the right time for a Reagan administration. In the aftermath of Watergate, people were looking for someone to heal the country. Even though Jerry Ford had already begun that healing process, people were clearly looking for the healing to come from the other party. Ford ran a very good race and nearly won in 1976, and in my view he was an excellent president. Nevertheless, the American public clearly believed at the time that we needed to do something different. Jimmy Carter came in with a strong appeal from his religious background, and the American public responded to that and elected him.

For all of his great qualities, I do not believe that Ronald Reagan would have been right for that 1977-to-1980 period. [He *end of paper* clearly was the right person in 1981, however. Whatever the reason—maybe God was taking care of this nation once again—he was the right person at the right time. Our country did get through the healing process in the aftermath of Watergate, and President Carter performed laudatory service in that regard, but by the time the 1980 election came along, it was apparent to everyone that he just was not governing very well.] President Carter suffered an ignominious political defeat at the hands of President Reagan because the country by that time was pleading for leadership. America did not want a healer, they wanted a fixer! President Reagan played the fixer role to the hilt, and he did it magnificently.

He was an outstanding communicator, which is also what the country needed at that time. Jimmy Carter was not a good communicator. In fact, the United States had not had a president who communicated well since John F. Kennedy, almost 20 years previously. JFK did not govern all that well, but in the brief period he served he had a unique way of communicating with the American public that is still recognized.

Aside from JFK, FDR was the only other able communicator of recent vintage. In 1981 the American public was ready for someone to say what he stood for, what he believed in, and what he was going to do to lead the country.

The country was ready for a real leader, and Ronald Reagan came in and led the country in 1981. Jimmy Carter did not lead the country—certainly not effectively. Jerry Ford will get modest marks for leadership, and Richard Nixon got excellent marks for foreign policy leadership, particularly in his first term, but Watergate tarnished it all in the second term. Prior to Nixon, Lyndon Johnson initially demonstrated good leadership for his Great Society programs, but then his success faded as he became caught up in the Vietnam conflict.

The country was hungry for effective leadership as it advanced into the decade of the 1980s, and Ronald Reagan provided that leadership. He had unique leadership qualities, and history will treat him well for what he accomplished.

Interestingly, Reagan turned out to be an effective *world* leader, although that was not his forte. He spent very little time on foreign affairs and did not know much about the subject. His instincts were awfully good, however. He was determined to handle the Soviet Union effectively, and he did so. Indeed, it probably took a Ronald Reagan to push the Soviet Union over the edge and bring about the fall of the Iron Curtain and the destruction of communism. Whether he thought through the strategy or whether he just acted on instinct, I am not sure. I suspect it was more the latter than the former. For whatever reason it worked and thus brought about the greatest foreign policy triumph since World War II.

Another interesting aspect of Reagan's foreign policy was his working relationship with his counterparts in the Group of Seven (G-7), especially with Margaret Thatcher. Reagan and Thatcher were a great team. The "Iron Lady" was the tough one of that duo who could dominate her colleagues around the world and, in fact, insisted on doing so. Ronald Reagan complemented her well. He was not an intimidating or domineering force. Rather, he persuaded people to his way of thinking by the force of his personality and the fact that people loved him. Together, the two of them dominated the G-7 summits and foreign policy generally because they were so cohesive and like-minded. Although they had totally different ways of imposing their wills on the rest of the world, with Reagan's soft touch and Thatcher's hard touch, together they achieved a great deal.

Reagan was helped in foreign policy by George Shultz, who was a respected and credible force in his own right, clearly one of the stronger secretaries of state we have ever had in this country. Having John Whitehead as the deputy secretary of state during that era was very helpful as well because his experience in the business world at Goldman Sachs trained him well for running the State Department. If the secretary of state is traveling around the world as most secretaries are wont to do and must do, someone has to "mind the store." Regrettably, we have often had situations in which the deputy secretary of state has not done that job well, and things begin to fall apart when a crisis erupts somewhere around the world. Our country was not in that position as long as John

Whitehead was the deputy secretary because he ran the State Department skillfully and represented the department exceedingly well in interagency debates.

* * * * *

Ronald Reagan's approach to domestic issues was very simple and therefore incredibly effective. The American public understood precisely where he stood. By contrast, the American public did not understand George Bush's position on domestic affairs, and President Clinton has exhibited great ambivalence and indecisiveness. The American public thus has not understood where he or his administration stands either, which was one of the reasons Republicans swept the congressional elections just a few days ago. People knew *exactly* where Ronald Reagan stood because he has had the same three or four major domestic policy planks all of his life. He talked about them in speeches endlessly, year after year, decade after decade. He believed in them deeply, and he could communicate those deeply held beliefs to the American public. Whether he was inordinately simplistic or really understood what was involved in those views, he led the American public down those paths, and he did it skillfully. The passage of the Tax Reform Act of 1981 was a good example of that leadership.

Another thing Reagan did very well domestically was carry the momentum of his electoral victories into the congressional process, enabling him to accomplish things quickly. George Bush was never able to translate electoral success into political activity on the legislative front. Bill Clinton tried, but he put all of his apples in the health-reform basket, which turned out to be a big mistake. That did not happen with Ronald Reagan, and he got a great deal done, particularly in his initial four years.

Reagan was uncompromising on his basic principles, and the American public respected that firmness. We now have a compromiser in the presidency, and the American public does not respect that trait, as was demonstrated by the elections last week. Since Ronald Reagan was such an effective communicator, the Democrats on Capitol Hill respected and feared him. They knew he could go over their heads and appeal to the American public anytime he wanted and do it effectively. They truly feared him politically, and at the same time, they loved him. Tip O'Neill was a classic example. He and Ronald Reagan disagreed on almost everything regarding public policy, but those two Irishmen had a wonderful relationship that lasted until Tip O'Neill's death.

In terms of running the administration, Ronald Reagan was a delegator, as anyone with his kind of personality must be. He wisely chose not to immerse himself in issues; Jimmy Carter, on the other hand, immersed himself in everything, even the use of the White House tennis courts. That was a terrible executive *modus operandi*. Ronald Reagan was at the other extreme, uninvolved in details. By and large, he did a good job of delegating, and he had talented people around him, which is why much was accomplished during his administration.

During my tenure as U.S. trade representative, which was basically the second term of the Reagan administration, I do not recall ever having a substantive one-on-one trade policy discussion with Ronald Reagan. The reason for that lack of discussion is because I obviously knew trade policy well, or else he would not have selected me for that job. He also had confidence in my ability, so there wasn't any need for his participation except where it was necessary to have *interagency* discussion at the highest level. In such cases, a number of people around the table would debate a key issue, and the President would ultimately make a decision. The policy-making process worked well, President Reagan knew it, and we accomplished a great deal on trade during the second term of the Reagan administration—probably more than in any other four-year period since World War II.

President Reagan came into office as the U.S. economy was on the verge of a recession. Interest rates exceeded 20 percent levels, the dollar went up and almost out of sight, we had lost our international competitiveness, and both the inflation and unemployment rates were in double digits. It was not a good time. Nevertheless, the troubles of the economy during the first two years of the Reagan administration were never blamed on the President, even though they usually are on such occasions. In this case the problems were attributable to what happened in the prior administration, and President Carter thus was blamed for them.

After 1982, the United States went into what was to become one of the longest-lasting recoveries in the history of the country, and that period really helped solidify Ronald Reagan's place in history. Approximately 20 million jobs were created during the

1980s, by far the best performance of any nation. Some additional problems emerged, however, such as large federal budget deficits, for which President Reagan must accept some responsibility. Our country experienced a major economic recovery, however, and the American public responded positively to it, though eventually there will be a price to pay by the younger generation as a result of the growing federal debt burden.

In dealing with the Congress, Ronald Reagan had the benefit of Republican control of the Senate from 1981 to 1986, which made a great difference. Nothing much happened legislatively during the 1986-to-1988 period. We did fight for and push through a trade bill in 1988, an effort in which I carried much of the load as U.S. trade representative because trade was such a high-profile issue. That ordeal became a huge brawl, but we got it done. It was probably the leading achievement of the last two years of the Reagan administration, but we spent endless hours fighting that battle. More than 200 conferees were named when the bill went to the Senate-House conference, probably more than on any piece of legislation until that time. Otherwise, not much happened in the last two years of the Reagan administration because control of the Senate shifted to the Democrats after the 1986 election. Everything went on hold, and that was the situation throughout the entire Bush presidency. Gridlock existed for a six-year period. Most of President Reagan's accomplishments took place in the first six years because of the leverage that Republican control of the Senate gave him.

* * * * *

The Bush presidency in my view was much less satisfactory to the American public, and it will go down in history as such. Obviously, President Bush was not in President Reagan's league as a communicator. Many other presidents were not either, but the contrast becomes vividly evident when one president is following another. That was a big hill for President Bush to climb. Inevitably, comparisons were made between the two, and President Bush was doomed to lose in those comparisons. He was not an inadequate communicator, but he certainly was not outstanding. He wasn't as inspirational as President Reagan, nor was he as motivational or as persuasive. He did not have a well-defined agenda, as did President Reagan. Many people sought to persuade President Bush to better define his agenda and demonstrate his vision for the country, but he just could not do it. He did not have the personality characteristics to accomplish that task; it wasn't natural for him, particularly on the domestic policy side. It was more natural for him on the international side, but even in that area his views did not come across to the American people as clearly as did President Reagan's.

Internationally, President Bush enjoyed tremendous credibility. President Reagan may have been more effective because of his strongly held and well-articulated views and his special relationship with Margaret Thatcher, but President Bush had immense international credibility because he knew all of the major world leaders on a first-name basis. President Reagan became acquainted with most of these people too, but he did not know them nearly as well as did President Bush, who had worked with many of those leaders for years. He knew their wives, their children, and their grandchildren. He had been to their homes. He probably had stronger personal relationships with his fellow world leaders than any president in U.S. history. It was a unique situation that we may never see duplicated. Knowing on a personal basis everyone in the world who counted in the foreign policy sphere paid immense dividends at the time of the Gulf War. No other human being could have put together the coalition that won the Gulf War. It was done in a matter of days by George Bush picking up the telephone and persuading other world leaders to collaborate and cooperate. That endeavor was truly one of the outstanding examples of American diplomacy in our history.

Domestically, he was not strong, however, and it showed in his body language. I used to watch President Bush in a press conference and I would cringe when he got to domestic issues because I knew his level of confidence was going to decline. In contrast, one could see his self-confidence soar whenever he tackled an international issue. He loved it. He would smile, his eyes would brighten, his voice would gain strength, and he would answer the question with firmness and without hesitation. The next question would be about the economy, and his shoulders would shrug. When Governor Clinton based his campaign on the theme, "It's the economy, stupid," he brought President Bush's weak spot to the fore, and that certainly did not help his campaign.

President Bush displayed phenomenal leadership qualities during the Gulf War, but he could not translate that into policy success after the war. Likewise, if one counts the number of chiefs of state who were in office at the time the Berlin Wall fell and are still in office, it is a very small number. Almost all of them have departed in the relatively short time since then and involuntarily, for the most part. The leaders of the Western world, including both President Bush and President Clinton,have not figured out what to do in the aftermath of the Cold War. Unless that situation changes in dramatic fashion under President Clinton in the next two years, American voters will again elect a new president in 1996. The United States is still going through a difficult learning curve on how to govern without a cold war. President Bush was unable to provide a post-Cold War vision for the United States, and he lost in embarrassing fashion in 1992. If President Clinton is unable to provide a post-Cold War vision, he too will lose ignominiously in 1996.

Leadership is being redefined, and I am not sure that Ronald Reagan would be the right person for this post-Cold War environment. We Americans have not yet identified that person, and most other countries have also failed to do so. President Bush had incremental portions of a vision, many of which were very sound, but he could not pull those portions together into a cohesive whole and explain it to the American public. President Clinton tried a different approach. He shifted from the incremental approach to a "grandiose" policy approach, which also has not worked. The question is, Where do we go from here, given that neither approach has succeeded?

Notwithstanding the difficulties that President Bush was having with vision, he would have won the election in 1992 if the economy had begun to improve a little sooner. It actually was improving when the people cast their ballots in November, but almost no one knew that. Favorable quarterly economic results came out a few days after the election, but they were too late to save him. Had Alan Greenspan and his colleagues shifted Federal Reserve policy three months earlier to get an additional one-quarter of economic recovery on the books, I think George Bush would be President of the United States today.

I want to say a word about first ladies simply because Barbara Bush redefined the role of a first lady in this country in a most commendable way. In my personal view, she was perhaps the most outstanding first lady of all time in terms of what the American public wants a first lady to be.

* * * * *

Regarding trade policy, NAFTA is working just as we had hoped it would. Ross Perot was totally wrong in his opposition, and the agreement will turn out to be a win-win-win situation for Canada, the United States, and Mexico. The numbers are already beginning to demonstrate that fact.

The Uruguay Round of the GATT negotiations is currently much in jeopardy, however. That agreement is far more important than NAFTA because it involves 123 countries rather than only three. The new trade engendered by the Uruguay Round is expected to add at least $500 billion a year to the Gross National Product of the world, and that is probably an underestimate. My guess is that it will be at least twice that number. The United States is likewise expected to benefit by at least $100 billion a year in additional output as a result of the Uruguay Round. I suspect that amount is also too low; it will probably be at least double if not more.

Nevertheless, the agreement is in jeopardy, which seems rather ironic under the circumstances. One of the reasons for the potential dilemma is the convoluted budget rules in Washington that require reductions in spending or tax increases to offset the reduction in tariff revenue as tariff rates are reduced. Given the dynamics of world trade, *more* tax revenue will actually be generated because of the additional economic growth that will result from this agreement. None of that is considered under the federal budget rules, however, because it is in the future rather than the present. The Clinton administration has thus been forced to find revenues to compensate for this shortage. The administration took several weeks before reaching its conclusions and thus jeopardized the whole agreement.

For that reason, a special session of Congress will be held in a few days to deal with an issue that should have been voted on months ago. The GATT Treaty is going to pass easily in the House on 29 November. When it comes up in the Senate on 1 December, however, it will be challenged under the Senate's obsolete, arcane budget rules, under which 60 votes are needed as opposed to the 51 necessary to pass the agreement itself. Unless 60 votes are found between now and 1 December, it will fail. That failure would mean it would then have to be voted on after the first of the year or it dies, which would be truly tragic.

Bringing it back after the first of the year, as Senator Helms suggested, is a very poor idea. The risk is that the so-called fast-track authority under which one must vote on the entire agreement no longer applies after the first of the year, which means that it can be amended. One can imagine what Congress will do if it has the privilege of amending this agreement, which would require taking it back and persuading the other 122 countries to agree with these amendments. As a practical matter, it would unravel. Therefore, the agreement needs to be passed on 1 December.

I was in Senator Dole's office last night and the Dole team is trying to decide how they can get over this issue. They know that they are going to be held at least partially responsible in the event it fails to pass, even though the old Senate will be voting on it rather than the newly elected Senate. Americans have either a historic triumph or historic tragedy approaching on the trade front in a few days.

QUESTION: Is the difficulty in passing GATT derived from the fact that Clinton will get the credit if it passes in this "rump" session of Congress and the Republicans are not anxious to see that happen? Is it domestic politics that is going to sabotage it?

MR. YEUTTER: Not any more, now that the election is over. That was the case prior to the election because Republicans were not in the mood to do President Clinton any favors, just as the Democrats torpedoed all of President Bush's legislation prior to the 1992 elections. In fact, the Republicans themselves are very concerned about it. The issue now is caught up in budget philosophy and to some degree in demagoguery by Ralph Nader and Ross Perot. In addition, some of our textile folks are trying to torpedo it through Jesse Helms, Fritz Hollings, and others. It is a combination of all of those things, but the domestic political issue to which you alluded has now disappeared.

QUESTION: I am interested in your idea that there are certain people for certain times in American political history. This subject is very interesting for those of us who study history as well as politics. Could you elaborate on what you think this country needs in the post-Cold War period we are in now? You alluded to the fact that we simply have not found the kind of person or persons to capture the mood of the American public in terms of where we should be going.

I happen to be from the Midwest originally, as you are, and I can remember how strong isolationism was in Michigan in the 1930s until Pearl Harbor. Could you speculate about how far the mood of this country could take us back to something that the British called "splendid isolation" in the 19th century?

MR. YEUTTER: I think we are at a bit of a crossroads right now—for the world and for the United States. One does not want to be too melodramatic about these things because our country is very resilient and somehow always manages to muddle through. Nevertheless, as I have stated in a number of speeches, I think this time is more critical than is generally recognized in America and perhaps around the world.

For example, I think the world is less secure today than it was during the Cold War. In the Cold War, most countries were lined up on one side or the other and everyone understood where they were. Now there is a great deal of confusion, and the American people are very ambivalent. They do not know whether our troops should be in or out of Bosnia, in or out of Somalia, or in or out of Haiti. They question whether our country knows what it is doing in its relations with China. People are apprehensive about the leadership of the world as a whole as well as leadership in the United States.

The United States has to take the responsibility of world leadership, because no other country can. Helmut Kohl is not going to make Germany become a world leader, although he may be the closest to this possibility. The Japanese would probably be the next logical choice, but they have a new prime minister every six months, so they cannot do it. They do not want to become world leaders anyway. The Russians are in complete turmoil. I do not know if anyone in Russia even knows who has their hands on the nuclear triggers right now, a fact that worries me enormously. One of the mistakes of the U.S. government during the latter part of the Bush administration and the beginning of the Clinton administration is that it did not get those ex-Soviet nuclear weapons "de-fanged." That should have been our country's highest priority, but we didn't do it, and too many of those weapons are still there. We don't know who is going to control those weapons five years from now.

At any rate, there are no prospective world leaders outside of the United States. Great Britain certainly is not going to accept that role; John Major will be lucky just to survive in office. The French are never going to assume a leadership role because too many people in the world dislike or distrust them. The United States must respond to the crying need for global leadership. In essence, no one is telling the world where it is going over the next 10 or 20 years. It has to be an American, and it has to be someone with an international vision.

From that standpoint, putting domestic issues aside for the moment, the world needs a Richard Nixon. He had the greatest international vision of anyone in my lifetime and perhaps of any president the United States has ever had. Henry Kissinger deserves much of the credit for Nixon's foreign policy successes, but I believe that Richard Nixon was the most important figure in formulating his administration's global vision. America needs someone with that kind of international vision, and not too many people in the world have an international vision, I am sorry to say. Dick Cheney may be a Republican presidential candidate in 1996, and of all of the potential candidates, I would say he has the strongest background in that area. Don Rumsfeld has a strong international vision as well, but he is not going to be a presidential candidate. On the domestic side a different set of leadership qualities is called for, and I do not know if one can find a person with both domestic and global leadership skills.

To illustrate how I interpret the election of last week, a Democratic businessman from Chicago said to me that the election results showed that the American people really believe they are overtaxed, whether it is true or not. He also said that the American people are fed up with government intrusion in their lives, and health care reform was just one example of this belief. People want less government and less regulation in their lives, he said, and it is about time that both Republicans and Democrats figure that out.

There is a lot of truth in what he said. The American public is frightened today. Americans do not like unsafe streets. They do not like unsafe schools. They don't like hundreds of thousands of Mexican immigrants coming into this country illegally, as shown by Proposition 187 in California. They do not like the value structure emerging in many places in this nation. They do not like it when single mothers with babies go on welfare rolls for years and years, and then their kids go on welfare rolls too.

We are in the middle of what I think is a major rebellion that has surfaced because the Cold War is over. Many of those issues were put on the back burner during the Cold War, and they are now on the front burner. Whoever is going to lead this country will have to respond to those issues or else get tossed out. The American public tossed out a president in 1992, fundamentally because the people did not believe George Bush was responding to domestic challenges. Americans also tossed out the Democratic leadership of the Congress in 1994 for essentially the same reason. I recently stated in a report to Hogan & Hartson clients that my personal view was that if neither the Congress nor the administration figures out how to respond to these problems in the next two years, they will both be tossed out in 1996. If people are fed up, Americans may end up with a Republican president and Democratic control of the House and Senate again, both for the same reason. We are in the midst of a volatile time, and the question is whether the leadership that people want to see will surface.

In that regard, a great deal of leadership will come from the incoming Republican House. Newt Gingrich, Dick Armey, and others are going to lead that body in a dramatically different direction. We will soon find out whether the American public likes it, but either way it will not be business as usual in the U.S. House of Representatives.

Last night I heard a presentation by Tom DeLay, one of the leaders of that group, and he told me they are going to roll out all of the legislation—their "Contract with America"—within the next 90 to 120 days. They will begin on 4 January and will be in constant session through the first 100 days, meeting on weekends if need be, with no time off for holidays. It is going to be an interesting 100 days. I do not know what the Senate will do, but on the House side, it is going to be the nearest thing to FDR's first 100 days the country has seen since 1933.

QUESTION: Did anything good come from the recent conference in Seattle on the Pacific Rim?

MR. YEUTTER: I think it was mostly fluff. It is nice to say that the Pacific basin nations are going to enact a free trade agreement by the year 2020, or that the developed countries of Japan and the United States are going to do so by 2010, but action speaks louder than words, and it is all words so far. All of this language about "historic achievement" is pure rhetoric at this point. No one has made a legal commitment to proceed; it is nothing more than a communiqué. Countries are a long way from an Asia Pacific Free Trade Agreement. It is good that they are being visionary, however. There is some symbolic benefit to all of this, but in terms of what will actually happen, the United States is a long way from a free trade agreement with Japan and a thousand miles, politically speaking, from one with China. We can't even get China into GATT, much less a free trade agreement. Many challenges lie ahead before that summit amounts to anything.

This administration wants to do grandiose things, and I wish it would just concentrate on doing business and running the country. If the administration wants to get something done in the Pacific Rim, it should go incrementally and start bilateral free trade negotiations with a number of countries there. The ASEAN countries (Association of South East Asian Nations) expressed an interest in getting this process going long ago during my tenure as U.S. trade representative. One can certainly visualize a free trade agreement with the United States, Singapore, Hong Kong, and maybe one or two other countries to get this process started.

QUESTION: Will those countries begin this process among themselves, whether or not we join? What about a pact with Japan?

MR. YEUTTER: Certainly there is a possibility, and indeed they have already taken some early steps toward forming a free trade agreement among the ASEAN countries. Whether they will do so with Japan is another matter; that is a long way off yet. The point is, countries must learn to do things incrementally. I expect that when the Latin American summit occurs in Miami, the same thing will happen. Those countries are going to talk about a Latin American or a Western Hemisphere free trade agreement—that will be the next thing. Instead of talking about a Latin American free trade agreement, why doesn't our country negotiate a free trade agreement with just Chile, for example? Chile has been waiting for one.

One of the problems that has put the Uruguay Round in jeopardy is that the administration overreached in requesting future fast-track authority. It asked for too much. If the administration had asked for fast-track authority on a deal with Chile four months ago, it would have gotten it in 30 minutes. If it had asked for fast-track authority that was limited to several Latin American countries or limited to finishing the Uruguay Round agenda, it would have gotten that as well. Unfortunately, the administration wanted full-scale fast-track authority to negotiate anything with any country in the world at any time over the next few years, and the Congress would not grant that authority. The administration jeopardized the entire Uruguay Round by pursuing grandiose such objectives.

QUESTION: After World War II, America emerged as the world's hegemon, economically. After the mid-1960s, our country went downhill. What do you think our international economic policies should be with respect to GATT and so on? Should the United States change its policies to allow more free trade or less free trade, more government intervention or less?

MR. YEUTTER: The answer today would be more free trade because the United States is so internationally competitive. Being that competitive, however, makes it easy to rationalize drawing a wall around the country and keeping competitors out, which is what the textile industry would like for us to do. Nevertheless, people need to look at trade from a national perspective, not on the basis of a particular industry. Overall, the United States is enormously competitive today. Americans grossly underestimate how competitive the country is. I sit on a host of corporate boards, and I can guarantee how competitive some of these American companies are. The United States has leapfrogged the Japanese and the Europeans over the last 10 or 15 years without anyone realizing it. A few years ago all of the magazines were writing about how Americans were destroying their manufacturing base and losing competitiveness and that our nation would soon be one of fast-food stores and no one would ever be able to find work in a factory again. At the very time those articles were being written, the restructuring of America was already well underway. The fact is, now the rest of the world is scared stiff of the United States! This country should open as many international markets as possible because of the opportunity thus provided to significantly increase U.S. exports. The United States is much more competitive than most Americans realize.

The Japanese presently realize that they are pygmies in competition with the United States in most products and services. They are frightened, and they should be.

For example, I serve on the board of Texas Instruments, a high-tech company. No Japanese company today can compete with Texas Instruments in most of its products—not one. I am also on the board of Caterpillar in the heavy equipment industry, where Komatsu was the big competitor a few years ago and was taking market shares away from Caterpillar. Today, Komatsu is not even close to Caterpillar; it cannot begin to compete. In fact, it is moving some of its production from Japan to the United States in an effort to restore its competitiveness. Caterpillar, by the way, is moving some of its production from Mexico back to the United States as a result of NAFTA—not the other way around.

Obviously, other countries are not going to sit still. They are going to recognize this trend and try to figure out how to leapfrog the United States in the next decade. The United States must continue to sustain its competitiveness, but as of today, it is far ahead and doing beautifully in a wide range of industries.

I can provide one specific example from Texas Instruments that relates to Federal Reserve policy right now. One of the reasons the Fed is tightening up on interest rates is that the rate of capacity utilization in this country is now 85 percent, which suggests that the United States is going to have higher inflation. My view is that the official capacity statistics are wrong because they are obsolete. Companies like Texas Instrument are adding new capacity in ways that do not show up in the numbers. In the last 18 months to two years, Texas Instruments has increased productivity so much in its existing plants in the United States and elsewhere that it has added to its existing capacity the equivalent of a billion-dollar investment in new plants. This boast in capacity does not show up in the Fed's numbers. That increase is spectacular and is one reason the United States is leading the world with its high-tech industries.

NARRATOR: Thank you very much, Mr. Yeutter, for your very timely and perceptive remarks.

CHAPTER 9

REALISM IN THE POST–COLD WAR ERA: THE REAGAN POLICIES*

STERLING KERNEK

NARRATOR: Professor Kernek was a visiting scholar at the Miller Center from 1987-88. He received his bachelor's degree at American University and his master's degree from the University of Western Australia. He studied in England with Professor F. H. Hinsley and earned a Ph.D. from Cambridge University in England. At Western Illinois University where he is a professor of history, he has proven himself the kind of faculty member that every university department hopes for, but few discover. He has been director of the honors program, a member of the committee that reformed the general education curriculum, and has carried out many other assignments with dedication and skill.

Professor Kernek has written widely on World War I, notably a book entitled *Distractions of Peace During War: The Lloyd George Government's Reaction to Woodrow Wilson, December 1916–November 1918.* He has authored articles on a range of subjects: Frederick Jackson Turner's frontier theory of history, Henry Kissinger, the comparative history of Australia and America, and Wilson's ideal of national self-determination. He is the author of an article in the *Virginia Quarterly Review* entitled "Historical Reflections on the Dangers Ahead" and in 1985 co-authored another scholarly paper

---

Presented in a Forum at the Miller Center of Public Affairs on 29 July 1993.

in the *Political Science Quarterly* entitled "How Realistic is Reagan's Diplomacy?"

We have asked Professor Kernek if he would help us better understand the role of one of the major points of view about foreign policy, specifically, realism in the post-Cold War era, as he traces it from the Reagan administration to the Clinton administration.

MR. KERNEK: To begin our discussion, I want to highlight some aspects of realism so that I can later make certain points. Realists argue that foreign policy is shaped by considerations of power and self-interest. Morality and ideals can provide guidelines or restraints, but considerations of power and self-interest predominate in the realist perspective.

Realists take a skeptical view of moralistic and idealistic justifications for policy. Moralism and idealism often strike them as either rhetorical camouflage for the pursuit of self-interest, or simply as bad statesmanship. This is not to say that realists are oblivious to moral considerations. They have written eloquently about moral dilemmas and tragic choices, but realists have doubts about harmonizing moral principles with the rough-and-tumble of international politics.

Some realist historians have been particularly hard on Woodrow Wilson for his alleged naiveté and excessively moralistic or idealistic policies. Others, myself included, have argued that Wilson was more realistic than his popular image. Realists are wary of the kinds of crusades Woodrow Wilson talked about, such as making the world safe for democracy. Their emphasis on the sovereignty of states has made them skeptical of the feasibility of international organizations such as the League of Nations. Realists also disliked Wilson's jaundiced view of balance-of-power diplomacy and his optimistic assumptions about the potential for international harmony.

Realists assume that international relations will continuously generate substantial conflict. They regard this as a mature expectation and are known for having a somewhat pessimistic view of human nature and of the nature of states in a competitive system. For realists, wisdom lies in maintaining stable balances of power. Most prominent realists favor moderation as a general approach to the conduct of diplomacy. Their favorite role models are 18th- and 19th-century European statesmen or the American Founding Fathers who understood how to manipulate power.

Among the most famous and influential American realists are Reinhold Niebuhr, Hans Morgenthau, Walter Lippmann, George Kennan, and Louis Halle. Morgenthau's standard text, *Politics Among Nations*, which first appeared in 1948, presented realism as a compelling theory as well as a guide to policy-making. By the 1950s, realism had become the dominant paradigm in international relations theory.

Realism resonated with popular attitudes in the post-World War II years. Isolationism and what were regarded as legalistic, moralistic, and naive efforts to promote peace between World Wars I and II had been discredited. The failure of the League of Nations, coupled with appeasement in the face of German and Japanese expansionism, had already focused attention on considerations of power and national security. The new threat of Soviet expansionism maintained that focus after 1945: Realism was used to justify the buildup of U.S. military strength as a means to contain the Soviets and establish a stable balance of power.

By the 1970s, a considerable body of criticism had developed. Realism has been faulted for having proponents who disagree among themselves, tenets that seem tautological, and key terms that are too broadly defined. Its focus on power is viewed as reductionist by many who emphasize interdependence in the international system. Realism's focus on states also diverts attention from transnational factors such as global movements in trade and technology. In addition, the paradigm's preoccupation with international competition slights the influence of domestic politics.

Despite these criticisms, realism remains the leading paradigm, partly because the writings of realists are usually more nuanced and subtle than their central theoretical propositions might indicate. Moreover, realism seems to help many of us identify key elements in complex events.

The current fashion, however, is to be suspicious of theories of international relations. John Lewis Gaddis recently wrote an interesting piece that chastised theorists for their failure to predict the end of the Cold War. In other words, if one cannot predict such a momentous event with any existing theories, what good are they?

When attempts are made to analyze the utility of realism, the expectations of what a theory can do must be held to modest proportions. I think realism works best, as Michael J. Smith has suggested, as a worldview. To insist that a theory must enable one to make predictions in order to be valid is to ask too much. If one wants a theory to shape research or to provide insights, then I think realism has lasting value.

Realism, of course, hardly guarantees a unified policy view among people who use the doctrine. In fact, the realists were divided on the specific reasons for opposing the war. Nevertheless, Vietnam was a remarkable case in which the founders of modern realism lined up in unified opposition to the war. I think they arrived at that position through their use of concepts that are central to realism. I will return to the significance of this in the discussion of the Clinton administration.

Ronald Reagan effectively invoked the rhetoric of realism in justifying his policy, especially in his first term. He justified a substantial military buildup in terms of not being naive about Soviet intentions—a weakness he attributed to Carter. Reagan spoke about the importance of power and strength in negotiations. These statements seemed to fit the rhetoric of realism. Realism really has a wonderful built-in public relations advantage. John Lewis Gaddis has described the use of the term *realist* as self-congratulatory. After all, who wants to be unrealistic? But there was more to it than that. I think Reagan was exploiting the attractiveness of realism and the continued influence of the doctrine.

Was Reagan a true realist? I think in some senses he was, but in other senses he was not. He was a realist in that military power was central to his conception of national interest. His succinct slogan of "peace through strength" certainly resonated with a great deal of realist writings. His initial plan was to spend $1.6 trillion in five years on the military—a staggering buildup. His condemnation of Carter was similar to realist condemnations of Woodrow Wilson. That also seemed to resonate with widespread views.

I think Reagan also could qualify as a realist in ways that would have appealed to Morgenthau. Reagan demonstrated— somewhat paradoxically, I emphasize—an acute sense of limits. He adjusted his negotiating strategy vis-à-vis the Soviets to help defuse the antinuclear movement that was flourishing early in his presidency. Reagan also altered his policy toward China. He originally had an old-fashioned pro-Taiwan policy toward China in his rhetoric, but he brought it quickly into line with the China policy of his three predecessors. He minimized direct military involvement in hot spots like El Salvador. The only military attacks he did launch were against weak states—such as Grenada and Libya—that offered easy victories. Likewise, when disaster struck the U.S. Marines in Lebanon, he promptly withdrew. Why, then, would I refuse to accept Reagan as a realist?

Reagan's Cold War rhetoric was simplistic and dogmatic. He was the type of cold warrior that Morgenthau and Kennan criticized throughout their careers. He displayed a monochromatic view of the world and framed most issues in terms of the Soviet involvement. His emphatic ideology was inconsistent with realism, which assumes complexity in issues and a desire for balance and restraint. Reagan also was far too optimistic to fit in with most realists. He appeared to believe that complicated problems could be overcome by bold and simple measures, even by nostrums. His tax cut was supposed to stimulate enough economic growth to offset initial revenue losses and thereby pay for the defense buildup. The Strategic Defense Initiative (SDI) held up Reagan's hope to overcome the moral dilemmas of mutually assured destruction and to render Soviet missiles impotent and obsolete. In spite of the program's inflated objectives, I must acknowledge, however, that SDI had a lot of practical domestic political benefits for Reagan, and initially it bolstered his leverage in negotiations with the Soviets.

Overall, Reagan deserves praise for his handling of the Soviets, so I cannot suppress a sense of irony when I mention criticisms. Yet, even in retrospect, he appears very optimistic and, at times, recklessly simplistic. He showed little or no concern that his efforts to promote the decay of the Soviet Union might provoke a dangerous response. The historical record has several dramatic examples of declining states that went down fighting or that resorted to foreign adventures to justify suppressing dissent or to stop the rot. What historian, Sovietologist, or realist would have thought that the Soviet Union would accept its demise peacefully? Paul Kennedy and John Gaddis were concerned about a violent last-ditch Soviet response. I also fretted about that possibility in an article I wrote for the *Virginia Quarterly Review* back in 1983.

Even more bizarre, Reagan had a romantic vision of huge reductions in strategic arms. Who could have predicted what a decade would bring? In a 1982 address to the British Parliament, Reagan called for a crusade for freedom that would leave Marxism and Leninism on the ash heap of history. His only concession to reality was that it would be a long-term crusade. Then communism virtually collapsed, and all of these things that had seemed dreamlike came true. People such as myself then went around talking about the role of luck in foreign affairs.

At the end of his presidency, basking in the glow of the Intermediate-range Nuclear Forces Treaty and the successful summits in Washington and Moscow, Reagan made many gushing remarks about Gorbachev. Although he qualified them with his "trust but verify" line, he fulsomely embraced Gorbachev, and in that too he was quite prescient. He had begun his presidency talking about Soviet leaders as people who would lie, cheat, steal, or do anything to promote communism. His subsequent (and remarkably transformed) perception of Gorbachev as a leader genuinely seeking accommodation now contrasts favorably with the contemporaneous views of professional analysts such as the CIA's Robert Gates.

George Bush remained somewhat skeptical of the change that was occurring in the Soviet Union. He lagged behind the curve early in his presidency, but he too adjusted to the startling realities of the Soviet collapse. He announced in May 1989—after a policy review of East-West relations—that it was "time to move beyond containment . . . and to seek the integration of the Soviet Union into the community of nations."

Bush remained at odds with U.S. allies regarding the amount of aid that should be extended to the Soviet Union, but his secretary of state, James Baker III, soon offered U.S. technical assistance in support of Soviet economic reform. Bush also reportedly prevented Robert Gates, who was then deputy national security adviser, from delivering a characteristically skeptical hard-line speech about Gorbachev's reform program. Then came several stunning events: the collapse of the Berlin Wall in November 1989, the emergence of independent governments in Eastern Europe, the collapse of the Warsaw Pact, the unification of Germany in 1990, the collapse of the hard-liners' coup in August 1991 followed by the total collapse of the Soviet Union a few months later.

Bush's lackluster, low-key prudence in this situation suited American foreign policy very well. Michael Mandelbaum noted that Bush did not embarrass, threaten, or provoke the Soviets, which convinced them that they could give up their empire in Eastern Europe without putting themselves in any mortal danger. Mandelbaum concluded, and I think correctly, that this restraint was the most important contribution to the events of 1989 that the United States was in a position to make. Bush's decision not to oppose German unification also can be justified on realist grounds. A realist argument could also be mounted on the other side, I suppose, but such is the nature of world politics and realist theory. Opponents of unification in Britain, France, and the United States were obviously troubled by the memories of what a unified Germany had wrought earlier in the century.

Bush maneuvered to minimize the danger of a unified Germany by keeping Germany integrated in the NATO defense structure. As Bush said at the end of his presidency, we encouraged a united Germany safely within the NATO alliance. The unification of Germany within the U.S.-dominated defense structure helps to preserve U.S. influence in Europe because Germany's neighbors have a major security reason for preserving American involvement. Two realist concepts in operation here are the drive for power and the balance of power.

Meanwhile, the Soviet Union had cooperated with Bush in his triumphant handling of the Persian Gulf crisis of 1990-91. Displaying great diplomatic skill, Bush won acclaim for the one-sided and quick victory. The only substantial domestic criticism was that he ended the war too soon—leaving Saddam Hussein in power. A realist defense of end-game decisions action can be mounted on the grounds that Bush wanted to preserve a regional balance of power. If Iraq had disintegrated, Iran might have become too strong and the hapless Kurds could have become even more troublesome, especially to our Turkish allies.

Bush liked to speak of his quest for a new world order. In a speech to the United Nations General Assembly in September 1991, he said: "As democracy flourishes, so does the opportunity for another historical breakthrough of international cooperation." Yet he displayed a keen sense of limits. Indeed, when facing the international crisis of the breakup of Yugoslavia, Bush demonstrated what might be characterized as realistic flexibility in the new world order. This was painfully true in the Bosnian crisis; he stayed out of it.

Likewise, Bush can claim a realistic rationale with regard to China in the aftermath of the June 1989 Tiananmen Square massacre. American ideals and support for democracy and human rights clearly were subordinated to geopolitical and economic considerations in that instance.

Bush tried to explain the zigs and zags of his policy with a balanced blend of idealism and self-interest. The approach was not inconsistent with realism, although in some instances I think it smacked of Wilsonianism. This was illustrated at the end of his presidency when he delivered a speech at Texas A & M University to promote the idea of American world leadership and to warn against isolationism. He alluded to America's withdrawal into isolationism after World War I and viewed the task of U.S. leadership as that of winning democratic peace for the world. Sounding at that point remarkably Wilsonian, he said: "The end of the Cold War has placed in our hands a unique opportunity to see the principles for which America has stood for two centuries—democracy, free enterprise, and the rule of law—spread more widely than ever before in human history." Bush added that "for the first time, turning this global vision into a new world, a better world, is indeed a realistic possibility. It is a hope that embodies our country's tradition and idealism which has made us unique among nations, and uniquely successful, and our vision is not mere utopianism." Then he invoked a realist rationale. "The advance of democratic ideals," he said, "reflects a hard-nosed sense of our own, of American self-interest. For certain truths have, indeed, now become evident: Governments responsive to the will of the people are not likely to commit aggression."

Various scholars (including Gaddis) have lent credence to this argument. Indeed, a consensus has emerged among scholars—backed by substantial historical evidence compiled by Michael Doyle and others—that democracies are, in fact, unlikely to go to war against other democracies. James Chace recently cited this conclusion in a chapter appropriately entitled "The Realist Vision." It seems ironic that the Wilsonian vision now is becoming part of the realist canon.

Striking another Wilsonian theme, Bush went on to argue that the global spread of free markets will help sustain American prosperity. "In short," he concluded, "by helping others, we help ourselves." Bush also asserted that restricting the spread of weapons of mass destruction is a vital U.S. interest, especially for young people. That passage might strike some Bush watchers as somewhat ironic in the light of the permissive attitude early in his presidency toward technology sales to Iraq and Pakistan. To his credit, however, by the end of his presidency he had tightened the flow of technology to those countries.

In a speech delivered at West Point in January 1993, Bush offered guiding principles regarding military intervention. While arguing that idealism "need not be at odds with . . . interests," he emphasized that principle does not "displace prudence." He said that the United States should not seek to be the world's policeman, although it should continue to exercise leadership. Bush's prudence and sense of limits was evident in a reference to the former Yugoslavia. He said, ". . . Up to now, it has not been clear that the application of limited amounts of force by the United States and its traditional friends and allies would have the desired effect, given the nature and complexity of the situation." Lawrence Eagleburger forcefully makes that point wherever he goes. Bush's prudence in dealing with what he acknowledged as Serbian aggression drew a great deal of criticism. William Safire, for instance, while admiring certain elements of the speech, wrote that Bush's "prudence still outweighed his principle" and that Bush "drew no lessons from his appeasement of dictators or delay in dealing with anarchy and Balkan aggression."

Clinton, during the election campaign, was also critical of Bush's prudence in regard to Bosnia. Nevertheless, Clinton has, in effect, followed his predecessor's lead, a pattern that is common in the history of the American presidency. During the campaign, Clinton scored points by assailing Bush's reticence toward Bosnia and also by advocating a more humane and principled approach in dealing with Haitian refugees and Chinese repression. It is now quite clear that Clinton has adopted Bush's policy toward Haiti. Clinton also has extended Most-Favored-Nation (MFN) treatment to China. After a flurry of threats in April 1993 to arm the Bosnian Muslims and attack the Serbs from the air, Clinton backed off in the face of European opposition. These policy adjustments give Clinton a considerable claim to prudence.

I believe in some ways we will find that realism resonates more than ever with recent trends in international policy. One might look back to the 18th and 19th centuries and examine the statesmen whom the realists have traditionally admired. Many of the concepts and techniques they used to promote peace and to maintain international stability involved elements of cooperation. The Concert of Europe is one example of such cooperation. The most successful efforts to use concert diplomacy to control crises in the 19th century were rough-and-tumble affairs, such as the containment of the Greek crisis from the 1820s to the early 1830s, the 1830 Belgian crisis, and the second Egyptian crisis during the years 1839-40. The great powers sometimes quarreled; certain powers opted out of joint action; and France in 1840 even seemed momentarily ready to fight to prevent joint intervention. In short, concert diplomacy was intermittently chaotic.

If the American public could be brought to understand that the international state system probably cannot perform any better than that, Clinton could avoid a lot of debilitating criticism. Lowering expectations while pursuing constructive international cooperation is consistent with his approach as a politician. Clinton wants the United States to work at international problems, but he wants us to do it in a mature way and pay as we go. To succeed, he must promote the realization that the outcomes will not be fully satisfactory or give us all that we may want.

NARRATOR: We have four people here whom we have invited to ask questions or make comments. These individuals have been involved for a good part of their career in thinking about these subjects: Professor Norman Graebner is familiar to all of you at the Miller Center; Brian Menard has just survived his Ph.D. examination; Professor Enno Kraehe is certainly among the top three scholars—if not the world's leading authority—who have written definitive works on Metternich, who was a kind of realist himself; Jean Marie Ruiz, in the line of French thought that begins with Raymond Aron and continues with his most direct associate, Pierre Hassner, has taken up a study of European and American realism. He is working with several of us here at the University of Virginia.

MR. GRAEBNER: In my study of realism—and all of my writings reflect a realist point of view—I have not experienced the problems that you suggested at the beginning of your presentation. I think a great mistake is made by many critics of realism who argue that Morgenthau and others have emphasized power and self-interest. In fact, it seems to me that in Morgenthau's writings there is very little on power and self-interest. His writings deal largely with how one succeeds in minimizing trouble in a world of sovereign nations. His emphasis is on keeping the peace, not on fighting wars. It therefore seems to me that when one deals with realism, one must recognize the fact that it deals not only with means—that is, with power—but also emphasizes *ends*. Realism entails the clear definitions of interest, danger, and the possibilities of a nation's foreign policy—all of which must be kept in some kind of balance.

I wrote an essay for a Naval War College conference that examined the 20th century problems of America in coming to terms with reality, which sometimes meant overplaying some enemies while underplaying others. We certainly underplayed Hitler and I think we overplayed Stalin. It is that search for a balance between ends and means that is realism. It is the search for reality—to examine world affairs and find out what is real. That is difficult to do, but it is not impossible.

Within this context I can understand why, if one puts all of these things together into a realist mold, a George Kennan and a Hans Morgenthau and all of the rest of us had our doubts about the Vietnam War. The problem in that situation was not about power. If you can mount a D-Day invasion in 1944, you can certainly mount the power to win a war in Southeast Asia against a little nation ten years old. The problem in Vietnam was in defining our national interest and defining the possibilities within the realm of those interests. It is on that basis that many realists criticized the Vietnam War.

MR. KERNEK: In Vietnam, it was considerations of power—how much power, what means of power are appropriate, what power does the other side have—that guided the realists. That is the distinction I am making. The realists put at the center of debate considerations of interest and power, while considerations of ideals and principles were placed on the periphery.

MR. RUIZ: Why is realism used by presidents? Has realism become standard in the bureaucratic process or because of the

influence of the advisers?   Do you think that the presidents—
because they are in power—realize that there are certain realities
that they cannot escape?

MR. KERNEK: I think realism has been such a dominant paradigm
that it has become a part of the political culture—what Brian
Menard would call the public philosophy, perhaps.

MR. GRAEBNER: Does this mean that realism actually informs the
practical actions and decisions of the people who exercise power?

MR. KERNEK: People whom I have talked to who have witnessed
foreign-policy formulation close-up would probably say no. For me,
as an academic, realism shapes the debate and the discourse about
it. Historians would like to think that policymakers use lessons
from history, but history is way down on the list of things that they
actually consider.

QUESTION: Do you think realism is here to stay, or might the
United States return to idealism?

MR. KERNEK: I must admit that a return to idealism is a strong
possibility. It seems that when people have tried to use realist
discourse, idealism has been the reaction. After Kissinger, for
example, came Jimmy Carter and human rights. Lawrence Eagleburger has spoken about the success that the Congress of Berlin had
in temporarily solving the Balkan problem in 1878. What followed
that episode was Gladstone's Midlothian campaign in Britain, in
which he staged a political comeback, talking about the betrayal of
principles and human rights among other factors. There often
appears to be an oscillation or swing of the pendulum between
realism and idealism. Let me add, however, that it is a distortion
of realism to say that realists ignore ethical considerations. I think
the writings of Morgenthau and Niebuhr are rich in their discussion
of policy dilemmas that would get us beyond the current level of
discussion. But there is always that simplistic appeal—the rhythmic
return to Wilsonian idealism. I should perhaps have said *so-called*
Wilsonian idealism, because I think Wilson has been greatly
misunderstood.

MR. RUIZ: Do you think realism can evolve into something different? I think we have to make a distinction between various periods and trends in the tradition of realism. In the late 19th century, for example, realism was not very prudent because it stemmed from the German tradition of realpolitik. Many Americans use the word *realpolitik* vaguely, but for me, it is associated with the Bismarck tradition. I would be glad to hear your opinion.

MR. KRAEHE: Actually, the term *realpolitik* was not Bismarck's invention, but a liberal one. Philip Rocol, a liberal, in 1852 looked back on the 1848 revolutions and asked, "Where did we go wrong? Why did we lose? Why were the revolutions unsuccessful?" The answer was that the revolutionists had failed to identify the levers of power. They had contented themselves with aimless theoretical debates about the "Good Society." In the meantime, the forces that commanded armies and bureaucracies gathered strength for a comeback. The liberals then adopted a policy of realpolitik that I would translate into the American idiom as "practical politics," as opposed to "tilting at windmills."

I would suggest that in the debate between realism and idealism in the United States, the function of realism has been to educate the American people in what constitutes competent foreign policy as opposed to idle daydreaming and wishful thinking. I have a hunch that this dichotomy or debate eventually will fade away as we cease to worry about whether a particular act is realistic or idealistic.

MR. MENARD: Is there a realist argument for U.S. military intervention in the Balkans?

MR. KERNEK: U.S. interests in Bosnia are limited. One must calculate how much power can be applied there consistent with our interests. We do have some interest in defeating Serb aggression because we want to discourage that kind of behavior in potential "Bosnias" elsewhere in the world. I have favored a policy of arming the Bosnians coupled with air strikes on Serb forces. I was dubious about other schemes that involved deeper involvement, but I think a realist argument could be made for doing so. Realists will disagree on fine points, but realism can frame the debate in terms of how much power to use and what the limits of our interest in that area are.

MR. KRAEHE: One possible development that would create a more concrete interest for us in Bosnia would arise if nations of the Muslim world embarked on a crusade to save the Bosnian Muslims. Bosnia would then have a magnified importance in the world, which we would have to consider.

MR. KERNEK: Kennan was right in the long run once before when he said that if you contain the Soviets, they will change eventually. Maybe he is correct in saying that the realities of worsening conditions in Bosnia will force us into action. I spoke of the pessimistic expectations of realists. It is always possible that the world situation will descend toward anarchy when one considers the implications of overpopulation. We now look at the spread of democracy, but one wonders if population growth could ever be effectively controlled in a democratic context. What pressures will give rise to authoritarianism? Obviously, there is tremendous potential for authoritarianism or fascism in Eastern Europe and the former Soviet Union. Nuclear weapons also are going to proliferate. Lowering expectations, therefore, may be a prudent step for the Clinton administration.

NARRATOR: Brian Porter at the University of Wales has an even more pessimistic view than that. He has written a long piece on ethnicity. His thesis is that even with the rise of nationalism in the 18th and 19th centuries, rulers spoke the same language and had common interests. But if ethnicity runs rampant in the world today, there will be no community of interest. Ethnicity, as he sees it, could lead to the dissolution of any consensus and unity in the world. It is a dark and bleak picture.

COMMENT: A substantial body of thought has arisen in favor of supplying arms to Bosnia. It would not be easy, and it would take time. Many realists say such action is long overdue.

MR. KERNEK: I would not disagree with your point.

COMMENT: I am fascinated by the fact that rapid changes in global communication, which will influence how we look at world problems, have not been mentioned. Communication is here to stay, and it is not going to be restricted to any one country. We can all communicate, and that may be idealism.

NARRATOR: Are you equally optimistic about communications when you watch television?

COMMENT: I was really thinking about Reagan, who is an example of what can be done through the media. We have the ability today to know what happened around the world in the last hour, but what is being fed to us may not be exactly real. We need to find some way to know what is really happening.

NARRATOR: We have been delighted to have Professor Sterling Kernek with us again to talk on the subject of realism in the post-Cold War era, and we look forward to having him back again soon at the Miller Center.

ANNEX

CHAPTER 10

THE REAGAN PRESIDENCY*

JOHN T. CONNOR

President Ronald Reagan is now being talked about as our greatest president since President FDR. His friendly and positive leadership style has been impressive to most Americans, and his handling of the Russians is, many of us think, the right mixture of strength and reconciliation.

My own activities during the Reagan administration have been limited to being an active member of the Committee of Former Cabinet Officials, leaders in business and finance, economists and educators, chaired by Peter Peterson, set up to make recommendations to the President and the Congress on ways and means to get away from the practice of huge fiscal deficits, high levels of deficit financing, the rising national debt, and the ever-rising cost of servicing the national debt. After several years of efforts, we have accomplished absolutely nothing since we have yet to convince the one man who makes all the difference.

The fiscal policies of the Reagan administration seem to have been well summarized by David A. Stockman when he says in the concluding paragraph of his book, *The Triumph of Politics* (p. 411):

Those are the reasons why we're *spending 24 percent of GNP,* compared to *raising only 19 percent of GNP in taxes.* They are also the reasons why the White House and the Republican party

---

Connor, John T. "Presidents I Have Known," in The Virginia Papers on the Presidency, *Vol. XXIII, edited by Kenneth W. Thompson, 16-17. Lanham, Md.: University Press of America, 1987.*

should *not* have told the American electorate in 1984 that we
don't have to raise taxes. It wasn't true.
(Emphasis added)

That fiscal deficiency may well prove to be the Achilles heel of
President Reagan, just as the Vietnam War was for President
Johnson. Yet the living legend of Ronald Reagan continues to grow
and grow. He still is just about the most popular President we've
ever had. Even those who disagree with him on the issues all like
him as a person; and all agree that no one could have handled his
shooting and cancer experiences with more courage and grace. In
spite of the growing economic problems, it looks as if President
Reagan will be fortunate enough to be able to retire to his ranch at
the end of his second term while still retaining broad public acclaim.
As Mr. Justice Holmes has said—legends are more important than
facts!